CAMOUFLAGED
SISTERS

Revealing Struggles of the
Black Woman's Military Experience

CAMOUFLAGED SISTERS

Revealing Struggles of the Black Woman's Military Experience

LILA HOLLEY

& 13 Courageous Sisters In Arms

purposely
created
PUBLISHING

CAMOUFLAGED SISTERS

Published by Purposely Created Publishing Group™

Copyright © 2015 Lila Holley

ALL RIGHTS RESERVED.

Printed in the United States of America

ISBN (ebook): 978-1-942838-49-4

ISBN (paperback): 978-1-942838-48-7

Special discounts are available on bulk quantity purchases by book clubs, associations and special interest groups. For details email: sales@publishyourgift.com or call (888) 949-6228.

For information logon to:
www.PublishYourGift.com

PRAISE FOR CAMOUFLAGED SISTERS

Lila writes with compassion and understanding as she takes your hand and gives you a glimpse of the life military women face. The daily struggles are poignant! This is a must-read for every woman considering military service and for every leader who wants to empower women of color.

-- Alice Gallop West, SGT (E-5)
US Army, 1985-1992

The world of female Veterans is a difficult one to travel. This book will take you into the minds of the women that have been there and done that from the beginning of their careers. Our American society somehow still doesn't know the lives they had to live. You must read this book and see military life from their point of view.

-- Dennis Ford Jr.
US Marines

I highly recommend this book to all women working in a male dominated profession. It is insightful, empowering, and encouraging to know that you can be successful and make it through challenges.

-- **Connie Daniels**, SSG (E-6)
Former US Army

Lila Holley is bold enough to highlight and tap into the untold stories of the African American Female Service Member in *Camouflaged Sisters*, a behind the scenes glimpse into the struggles and challenges that these women faced as they navigated through the male dominated military organization. A great read; certain to get people everywhere talking in a way that can change lives, both personally and collectively.

-- **LaMeka Grayson**, CPT (O-3)
Retired US Army Reserve

The title alone is intriguing. These women are layered with not only the physical camouflage all Soldiers wear, but the "uniform" Black women have had to wear just to fit in this democratic society. Add the camouflage a sister wears as a Soldier and wow! That makes this book a must read for Veterans like me and our young sisters currently serving. Thanks, Lila Holley, for dealing with this issue at this time and gracious space.

-- **Karen Maxfield-Lunkin**, CPT (O-3)
US Army (1984-1990)

As a Black female Veteran, I experienced my share of ups and downs during my military career. I was looking to find myself in one of the *Camouflaged Sisters* stories. I love that there in now a book about and for Black Female Veterans. Thank you all for sharing your story.

-- **Trina T. Powell**, E-4
Former US Army Military Police

I served in the military for over 20 years with men and women from many different backgrounds and nationalities around the world. I am proud to know that *Camouflaged Sisters* will provide a more in-depth perspective to how these courageous military women and now authors share their experience with the world.

-- **Sylvester Ryan**, SFC (E-7)
US Army Retired

TABLE OF CONTENTS

ACKNOWLEDGMENTS

There are so many people to thank for their support and their encouragement over the years, even to this day.

I choose to take this opportunity to thank the Women, my Sisters, who have joined me on this journey. Many of them are first-time authors. All of them wear multiple hats – wife, mother, entrepreneur, volunteer, and community leader to name a few. Regardless of their many responsibilities, they found the time to gather their thoughts and find the right words with which to tell their story.

I applaud each of you, Ladies, for your courage to tell portions of your story that were difficult to relive, emotional to recall, and tucked away deep inside because they are not often shared. Your story will help many coming behind us, especially our fellow Sisters in Arms. They will read your words and remember them in their times of need. They will take into consideration your advice on the importance of finding *Balance* while serving. They will heed your warning of staying true to yourself when faced with *Leadership* challenges. These Sisters will lean on their *Faith* when times get tough and others look to them to be that "calm under pressure" leader. They will read our words about the good, the bad, and the ugly of *Mentorship* and strive to be a Mentor who makes a difference in the lives of the next generation of leaders. These Sisters will prepare for all *Transitions* that will occur throughout their military careers and lives and tackle each of them with poise and grace.

I thank YOU, my Camouflaged Sisters, for your encouragement, prayers, dedication to this project and to each other, and, most of all, for your Sisterhood.

Amanda Randolph

Sylvia McCrea

Tamara Sanford

Catrena Findley

Patricia Watts

Sinceria Allen

Vernessa Blackwell

Shirley LaTour

Lenita Cornett

Kathy Marie Carter

Keisha Moulton

Luvina Sabree

Keshia Hughston

FOREWORD

By Marticia Williams, SGM (E-9)

Leadership, I never really gave it much thought. Little did I know, I was being groomed and strengthened to serve at the top of the NCO leadership ladder of the United States Army from a very young age. As the oldest of seven children, leadership was something that was very natural to me. It's just something that usually falls on the eldest child. With leadership instantly came the sense of responsibility. It was because of that thought pattern of being responsible for others that I would be recognized throughout my 26 years of military service. The funny thing is that I don't recall regularly hearing what a great leader I was from the men I served with.

As a Black female leader who has lived the Black experience, I am very multi-culturally aware. The truth is, women have contributed awesome examples of great leadership throughout military history. For a long time, Black women have and will continue to take the lead in leadership roles that have greatly contributed to the success of this country and this world. We see a shift in our military leaders today as more opportunities are made available to women serving.

But there is still more work to be done. When women leadership achievements, accomplishments, and contributions are made a priority and displayed as training tools, then women will receive the earned recognition they deserve.

As a female Military Police Officer, I encountered doubt in my ability to accomplish my tasks to the same standard as my male counterparts. I felt the need to prove myself, so I set high standards of performing for myself. Going above and beyond became my modus operandi. This behavior fed my leadership style and, in three short years, I was promoted to Sergeant. I was on my way to serve at the top leadership rank in the military police corps.

It was by no means an easy road to travel to become Sergeant Major (SGM). During my time as a drill sergeant at the US Army MP School, I experienced a unique set of challenges. I realized that my male counterparts really did not consider females, specifically Black females, as competition in the race for promotion selection. They clearly had no idea the path that I was on. As I prepared for my promotion board, I noticed there were strong female leaders, but they were few in numbers. This was when I realized I was missing out on some critical mentorship from another female, a Black female leader.

While I acknowledged this lack in my career, I did not let this stop me or hinder my journey. I was promoted to SFC then to MSG, and assigned as a First Sergeant. While attending the Sergeants Major's Academy, I was promoted to SGM and earned my masters degree. My last assignment was as the Provost SGM for the largest military installation, Ft. Hood, TX.

I would have to say that many of my struggles mirror those of other female leaders in the military, especially the women in *Camouflaged Sisters*. Leadership challenges and the lack of mentorship from other Black female leaders plagued me during my career. While my faith sustained me every step of my journey, I also experienced challenges with balancing family life while climbing the ranks. And even though I retired on my own terms, I still struggled in transition when I left the military. I felt as though no one really understood the challenges I had faced over the years.

This book is a must read and a definite conversation starter. *Camouflaged Sisters* is a book that is very much needed at this time in our military history. As women continue to break barriers and experience more opportunities to serve in greater capacities, Black women must continue to fight to be heard. We cannot continue to suffer in silence. My hope is that this book gives courage to those Sisters in Arms who felt like their voice had no power for so many years.

I salute you, my courageous Camouflaged Sisters.

Marticia Williams, SGM (E-9)
US Army Retired

INTRODUCTION

Some would have you believe that women are the weaker vessel. Granted, some of us may be less physically endowed than some men, but *weaker vessel?* I cannot agree with that label.

Women have made history by showing their strength during challenging times. Often times, it only took one woman to influence a movement or create a world of change for those around her and for generations to come. This strength often comes in times of oppression or as a means of survival. I think of women like Helen Keller, Rosa Parks, Malala and even Oprah Winfrey who broke the mold of "normal" and created immeasurable opportunities for women today.

This act of breaking molds, knocking down limitations, and creating opportunities extends even into the military, where women make up nearly 14.5% of the Armed Forces. Women like Cathay Williams broke down barriers that prohibited women from enlisting into the Armed Forces, although she had to pose as a man to get into the Army. Once she was in, however, she broke down the stereotypes that women were not capable of serving in the military.

CAMOUFLAGED SISTERS

Over time, women have proven themselves to be invaluable members of the Armed Forces. Black women, who have been among the last ethnic/gender group to make significant strides in the military, continue to show themselves worthy of the accolades enjoyed by their male counterparts over the years. These women were among the firsts, creating opportunities for generations of Black women, like us, to come behind them and enjoy successful military careers:

1. Reverend Alice Henderson – July 1974: the first female, Black or White, commissioned as a chaplain in the military

2. Hazel Winifred Johnson – September 1979: the first Black Woman promoted to the rank and position of Brigadier General, Chief of the Army Nurses Corps

3. CSM Evelyn Hollis – April 2004: the first Black female Command Sergeants Majors (CSM) of a combat arms unit

4. Major General Marcia M. Anderson – the first Black female Major General in the Army Reserve component; October 2011: assumed the position of Deputy Chief, Army Reserve (IMA) with duty at the Pentagon

5. Admiral Michelle J. Howard – March 1999: the first Black woman to command a U.S. Navy ship; today she serves as the Vice Chief of Naval Operations; the first Black woman to hold this post and in 2014 she became the first Black female to achieve the rank of four star general; she holds the highest rank by a Black woman in any branch of service

6. Colonel Meryl Tengesdal – One of eight female pilots to fly the Air Force's U-2 aircraft and the only Black female in history to pilot the aircraft

Even today in 2015, women continue to make history in the military with the first group of women entering the U.S. Army Ranger School, which boasts of a success rate of only 42-65% graduates among the men that attend. Women have proven they are strong and bring so much talent to the table. Despite the broken ceilings, Black women still have more work to do and we cannot get comfortable just yet. Military Regulations governing natural Black hair and women's hairstyles are still being argued in the Pentagon, while the Department of Veterans Affairs has made Women's Health (to include Mental Health) and compensation for Sexual Military Trauma a priority among their top issues to address.

CAMOUFLAGED SISTERS

In the chapters that follow, you will meet women who have served our country honorably in the Armed Services. These women are part of a rich history. They are the living legends of the women listed above who came before them. They gladly take the torch and run with it as examples of excellence in leadership, mentorship at its finest (or not), and immeasurable strength. You will read stories of mentorship done incredibly well, offensively bad, or altogether absent; faith that pushed them through trials; strength and perseverance in the face of challenges; and victory over difficult situations as they fought to find their voices in order to share their stories.

We salute you Camouflaged Sisters – time to reveal YOUR Stories of Triumph!

Coach Lila

TRANSITION

"You gain strength, courage, and confidence by every experience in which you really stop to look fear in the face...Do the thing you think you can not do."

- Eleanor Roosevelt

1

Standing Strong While Enduring Constant Change

LILA HOLLEY

'm always ready to share my military experiences with anyone who will listen. I served for 22 years, and I was blessed to live in and travel to some amazing places across the globe. Yes, there was an immeasurable amount of sacrifice involved with choosing a military career, but the good outweighed the bad, and I would choose to do it all over again. I came from humble beginnings – I am the oldest of six kids and was a teenage mother. The military allowed me to provide for my family in ways I couldn't image as a 15-year-old pregnant Black girl from the hood.

Throughout my career, I learned so much about myself and feel I am better for the experience. During my 22 years, I saw and experienced a lot of change: I went from lower enlisted to NCO to Warrant Officer; I went from being a single mom to being married dual-military; I went from living in the continental U.S. to living in paradise in Hawaii to being deployed to places like Bosnia, Iraq and the Philippines. Yes, a lot of change, but through it all, one thing remained the same – I was a Black female in a White male-dominated career field. Though I was reminded of this fact every day, I did not allow it to limit me or stop me from setting big goals for myself and achieving those goals. I didn't allow it to make me compromise who I was as a person.

Women who go into male-dominated career fields often face many challenges, such as discrimination, harassment, lack of promotion opportunities, being ostracized for "motherly" duties, or viewed as too "emotional", to name a few. While I had my own share of challenges, I worked through them to experience success in my military career. In the process I learned several lessons. Here are three of the toughest lessons I learned as a Black woman in the military:

1. To the Moon, Soldier!

I felt the need to set astronomical standards for myself throughout my military career. Why? Because as a Black woman in this White male dominated, masculine career field, you can get rolled over, dismissed, overlooked, rejected, minimized, or ignored. I was not about to let that happen. I needed to be taken serious and recognized for the assets I bought to the team.

I recall being in a Warrant Officer Advance Course in a class discussing affirmative action and if it had any bearing on the promotion system. I remember a classmate, a White male, growing upset by the discussion and then he made a statement, "It's not fair that someone would get promoted merely based on the gender or the color of his or her skin." I thought to myself, was he even listening to the block of instruction? The military DOES NOT promote ANYONE who is not deserving of promotion. This meant I had to meet the same standards as any one of my many White male counterparts going up for promotion; I didn't have an edge up because I was a Black female.

It was because of attitudes like this that I set such high standards for myself. There were so many times I was the only female or the only Black person in the meeting, briefing, in the office, or on the staff. I began to grow accustomed to this and began to measure myself against my White male peers. In my mind, that meant having to be 10 times better at my job, to be more poised and professional, and to speak a little louder in order to be heard. I mastered the art of controlling my emotions and being that "calm under pressure" leader my supervisors needed. As a result, I lived with an inherent level of stress that became normal and was sometimes needed for me to thrive in my career.

What was the real cost of functioning like this? I became my own worst critic. I became a perfectionist, I didn't take or give constructive criticism very well, and I never felt as though I slowed down enough to truly enjoy the rewards of my success. Through maturity over time, I eventually learned to enjoy the fruits of my labor and to accept myself – flaws and all. It was truly liberating when I was able to define success for myself on my own terms.

2. If You Think You're Lonely Now...

There are hundreds of thousands of people serving or who have served in the military, so how can the military be a lonely place for a Black woman? I felt this way for a major portion of my career. The higher up the rank structure I moved, the lonelier I grew. There was no one there who looked like me, no one to serve as an example, no one to reach out to for mentorship. I believe there is an extreme amount of power in having a living, breathing example with whom to compare yourself. That's why I believe President Barrack Obama's presidency will have a far greater impact on the Black community than any political legacy he will leave behind. Now little Black boys can truly dream of being the president of the United States because now they see it can be done by someone who looks like them.

This is how the military became a lonely place for me. Often times I was the only Black officer on the staff and the only Black female in the office. I often joked about being the only "little chocolate face" in the room during a briefing to the general or in a staff meeting. While I was able to joke about it, the lack of Black female representation had an impact on me. I can count on one hand the times I served side by side with another Black female Warrant Officer, and I must admit these moments were life changing for me.

The first time was when I was stationed in England and I worked for my first Black female Warrant Officer. I had just been promoted to the rank of Staff Sergeant and I guess she saw something special in me. It was her prompting that caused me to seriously consider becoming a Warrant Officer. I am so glad she prompted me, shared with me the pros and cons of being a Warrant Officer, and explained the process of submitting a packet. I submitted my packet and was selected in 1997. I never looked back or regretted making this important career decision.

The second time I served with a Black female Warrant Officer was during my first deployment to Bosnia. She immediately took me under her wing and showed me everything I needed to know about the operation and our responsibilities. Again, I felt as though she saw something special in me because she was very nurturing, patient, and took the time to teach me things. As a result, I not only became a better analyst, but I also discovered my leadership style because I saw it in action in her. She was smart, confident, detailed, focused, knowledgeable, encouraging, influential, and helpful. It was because of this encounter I was able to confidently walk into my own leadership style as a nurturing leader who truly cared about my Soldiers. There were times I was criticized for coddling my Troops but I never wavered from who I was as a leader because it worked for me - all thanks to the example I had early in my career.

The third time I served with another Black female Warrant Officer was at Fort Hood when my unit was preparing to deploy to Iraq. This experience was short but very impactful. I found out I was pregnant just days before I was to fly to Iraq, so I ended up on the Rear Detachment. One of our responsibilities was to in-process new Soldiers into the unit and prepare them for deployment. This beautiful Black female came to the unit as a result of my pregnancy, I have to assume, with such a positive attitude and willingness to do her duty that I immediately took notice. She was a mother and married to another Soldier just like me. I knew she would sorely miss her family during her deployment. She showed me that it was truly all about how you looked at things that made the difference in your military career.

When I later got the call from my Branch Manager to leave Fort Hood and deploy with another unit I remembered that lesson from this Sister. My daughter was only one year old and I knew I would miss her terribly. But I did not focus on that; instead, I focused on the positives: my family would be in New York closer to extended family, my husband would be in a unit that was not deployable so my daughter would have at least one parent there with her, and I would be able to get this deployment out of the way while she was still young and probably wouldn't remember it much. It was because of this attitude I adopted from this Sister that I was able to move forward in my career, filled with sacrifice and family separations, always outweighing the bad with the positive.

3. Triumph in Transition

My career was a continuous sequence of transitional events. I joined the military as a Private 2nd Class

(PV2) and retired as a Chief Warrant Officer Four, transitioning through eight rank promotions. I was a single mother of one young child when I joined and the mother of two children with an 18-year age difference when I transitioned out. During my career, I was half of a dual-military marriage and the sole military member in the family when I retired. During these transitions the greatest lesson that I learned was transitions are inevitable, so embrace them. I used these transitions as opportunities for personal growth while I embraced my professional growth. I was better prepared for the increased responsibilities that came with the promotions as a result. Having a positive attitude is key. I was able to remain flexible when my career path didn't follow my plans. This was key during my last 6 years of military service, during which I had to move my family 4 times.

Even in my transition from the military to civilian life, I continued to learn. I believe I learned the greatest lesson of all – I learned who I was. I learned to function and excel in this male-dominated career and reach a significant level of success, but at what cost? In my transition from the military, I discovered being that "calm under pressure leader" came at a cost. When I was forced to process the emotions I encountered as a result of leaving the military, I discovered I had developed an unhealthy manner of processing my emotions that resulted from all the many transitions I encountered in my life.

I think we can all agree that life transitions will bring about an emotional response. I knew this to be true, but in the military there was no time to dwell on the emotions of the transitions in my life. I had a job to do; there was no time to dwell on a break up with a boyfriend. There was a mission to accomplish and no time to stress over this month's bills. I learned to suck it up and figure something out quickly. I only began to notice a struggle with my emotions when I transitioned out of the military. I became angry and easily agitated, and I experienced difficulty communicating with loved ones.

I had operated in a high-stress, testosterone-heavy environment for so long that I had developed these aggressive emotions and personality traits as a way of surviving in the military. They were not needed at such a high level of intensity in my transition out of the military. I am a strong Black woman because of my military experiences. I accomplished things I really didn't know I could until I was faced with and conquered them. I know now that I don't have to be overly aggressive toward others, or in constant competition with others, or prove my worth or speak loudly to make an impact, unless of course the situation warrants it, and then it's Camouflage On!

As we came together on this project, we felt strongly about discussing mentorship among Black women in the military. We believed this topic was important to address in this book, not only from the Black woman's perspective but for all women in the military to understand that we must serve as our "Sisters' Keeper." At the end of each author's chapter, read how having a great mentor affected her military experience for the better or how the lack of a good mentor, female or male, affected her.

While our personal experiences with mentorship vary, you will notice that collectively we feel it is important to seek out good mentors throughout your military career. It's even more important for Black Women in leadership roles to take on the task of mentoring those young leaders coming up the ranks behind them, especially our Black Sisters in Arms. If a leader is unable to actively take on the role of mentoring others, she should be aware that in some way, shape, or form, an influential troop is watching and taking note of her behavior. Be advised and govern yourself accordingly, Leaders.

Here's my experiences and opinions on mentorship among Black Women in the military:

During your military career, did you ever have another Black woman as a mentor?

Yes, I was very fortunate to have a few Black female leaders in my life during my career. We may not have had an official mentor-mentee relationship, but they were very influential to me during my career. I recall one Sister who took on the role of a mentorship immediately in our relationship. She was an awesome example of a leader for me.

What was your experience like (or lack of experience) with a Black woman as a mentor?

My mentorship experience with another Black woman in the military was very positive and actually life changing. I had just transitioned from enlisted to Warrant Officer and was on my first deployment in Bosnia. I was so unsure of myself as a new officer, as a leader, and in my abilities as an analyst.

Seeing another Black woman in action in her leadership style reassured me that I didn't have to compromise who I was to be effective. She was strong but never overbearing or rude, smart but never condescending, and nurturing but never demeaning. Having her provide feedback, guidance, and constructive criticism reassured me that I possessed the talent needed to be successful. I truly valued that experience and that relationship blossomed into a beautiful friendship with CW4 (Ret) Amanda Randolph. I am so blessed to have her as co-author of this book with me.

What would you tell other Black women who serve about taking on the role of a mentor to other Black women serving?

I would stress how important it is for Black Women to serve as examples to others, especially to other Black Women in uniform. I always believed in the incredible power of having a living breathing person as an example to follow, something that is missing in many Black communities across America.

It's hard to see yourself as a rocket scientist if you've never seen one with your same skin tone. Great leaders come in all shapes, sizes, genders, and races. Black women should seek out the opportunity to break down negative stereotypes that we're angry, emotional, or can't get along, to name a few. We should seek to serve our fellow Sisters coming up the ranks behind us. If one succeeds, we all succeed.

2

Succeeding Against All Statistical Odds

VERNESSA BLACKWELL

Retirement is supposed to be happy and joyful, but I know firsthand how difficult it can be to break through the struggle of transition that we all have to encounter. We have accepted that this process will be a struggle for far too long. It is absolutely possible to overcome the barriers that keep you in a place where you have to struggle and, despite all your hard work dedication and achievements, you still don't feel rewarded.

With over 22 years of experience in leadership and training roles in the U.S. Army, I have gained expert knowledge of operational experience, personnel management, and cross-functional communication. I also have extensive experience in human resource, managing high-value equipment, leading teams, developing talent, and maximizing organizational efforts during complex projects and initiatives. Even with all my expertise, translating my experience in the military to civilian language has been an issue for me, as the civilian sector does not understand the military acronyms or the language that we have learned to use for so long. HOOAH!!!

Transitioning (or should I say retiring? I like that word a whole lot better) has been difficult for me. I started this process six months ago, and my retirement date is July 2016. I am so glad that I started early; it is a very lengthy process. It has been long and grueling for me. I am a dual-status employee for the Army National Guard, where I serve as a Senior Human Resource NCO. This process is a lengthy one because I have to make sure I have my National Guard Retirement Points (RPAS) correct as far as my time and service, as well as the time and service for my federal retirement. Once the process is complete, I will get two retirements, and that's great. I am now paying back into my retirement for my active duty deployments to make sure I receive credit.

My struggles as a Black female have been numerous, and I have had to struggle a lot throughout my career. I have been passed over for promotions and not selected for positions due to me refusing to sleep around. Also, the crab in the barrel mentality that a lot of folks have in the military is frustrating, too.

Crab mentality, sometimes referred to as crabs in the bucket, is a phrase that describes a way of thinking best described by the phrase "if I can't have it, neither can you." The metaphor refers to a pot of crabs. Individually, the crabs could easily escape from the pot, but instead, they grab at each other in a useless "king of the hill" competition that prevents any from escaping and ensures their collective demise. The analogy in human behavior is that sometimes claimed to be that members of a group will attempt to "pull down" (negate or diminish the importance of) any member who achieves success beyond the others out of envy, conspiracy or competitive feelings, although this is not the behavior being exhibited by the crabs simply trying to escape themselves, without any knowledge or understanding of the supposed "success" of their fellow creatures.

I have noticed that a lot of female Soldiers in the National Guard were on the fast track program. I find it safe to say a lot of them were dating someone in their chain of command. Many of them received promotions for favors, more or less quid pro quo, or "a favor or advantage granted or expected in return for something." I was deployed and in a majority male unit. There, I was reprimanded for going AWOL. I received a Red Cross message from home due to a family emergency. I was authorized 15 days of leave to come home and handle the situation. This occurred in the winter of 2003. When I was scheduled to fly out to return, no flights were allowed out. All flights were grounded due to inclement weather.

Because of this transportation issue that was beyond my control, I returned to Iraq two days later than I was supposed to. Even though I informed my 1SG and Platoon Sergeant of this situation, I was counseled and reduced in rank. I went from being a Sergeant back to a Specialist. At the time, I was number two on the Staff Sergeant list and due to be promoted any day. The same scenario occurred with a male Soldier that went home on emergency leave and did not return for 30 days. Yes, 30 whole days! His punishment was extra duty for 15 days. No loss of rank, no forfeiture of pay. How do I know this? We went before the Battalion Commander the same day. He actually went before me, I asked him what the decision was. I was also admin, so everything was routed through the S-1 Section. This is an example of one of my struggles in the military.

While non-military women are making a comeback from the recession, and even experiencing less unemployment than men, female military veterans are having a far harder time of making it outside the military. Not only are African American female veterans not easily bouncing back from the recession, but they also face many other obstacles resulting in more Black female veterans ending up unemployed and homeless.

In fact, according to a Forbes article written in 2011, "female military veterans are now twice as likely to become homeless than women who never served in the military." So why is this happening? Is it simply employment issues, or is the U.S. Department of Veteran Affairs (the VA) also a major source of the issues?

According to research conducted by the VA, almost one in every five women veterans has been delayed in receiving (or gone without entirely) needed care in the last twelve months alone. It is the conclusion of this research that has led the VA to believe that it needs to expand its delivery of gender-specific health care services to meet the needs of the rapidly growing number of women they serve – services such as gynecologists and mental health services.

In addition to healthcare, women veterans also experience difficulty being able to use and translate their military experience into civilian employment opportunities. It is very evident that this is at least one cause of the high unemployment rate concerning women veterans. This, coupled with the incredibly high rates of homeless women veterans, which is at least twice as high as women that are non-veterans, is a disturbing truth that needs to be faced head on. The inability to reverse these high rates will only serve to make matters worse. These are problems that must be addressed.

There are several obstacles to avoid and work around when attempting to transition into civilian life. Hopefully, knowing these obstacles will give future veterans a foothold on the transitioning process.

1. **Certifications:** While jobs outside the military emphasize the need for continuing education and advanced certifications, this is not something currently required in the military workforce. In some areas, a veteran may be overqualified for a job, but in many professions, certifications and degrees are the key to getting a civilian job.

2. **Translating Military Skills:** Many veterans leave active duty military thinking their skills will be easily used and/or understood by future civilian bosses, but instead, they find that their skills are not understood by civilian employers and they sometimes experience difficulty translating their skills into terms understood by civilian employers.

3. **Military Talent:** With the expanding role of military women in combat operations over the years, many civilian employers don't always understand the role of women in the military, which may become problematic. Many female veterans are having a difficult time translating their military experience, roles, and responsibilities to future employers. Many women feel insecure about whether or not a civilian employer will believe that they can do the tasks they have written on a résumé when all it says is "Army" as experience/background.

4. **Transition Program:** Another major issue is the lack of government transition programs, and the fact that the ones that do exist are severely outdated. According to an article written by USA Today, "The government's signature Transition Assistance Program hasn't been revamped since its launch nearly two decades ago" and that was in an era before there were the high numbers of women in the military like there are today.

These are some of the main issues that come up for transitioning female veterans, but they are serious enough to keep women from getting jobs and having homes. So, what are some preparatory actions that female veterans can take early on to help ease their transition into civilian work life? While we can't change what the government is slacking in by ourselves, there are some suggestions of actions we might take on our own that could help.

1. As you prepare for transition, research the jobs you are interested in and what certifications are necessary, including extra certifications, and go after them. Look for ways you can use your military training and experience to apply them toward obtaining the important certifications needed for the job.

2. "Speak civilian." Translate your military skills into terminology that civilian employers will understand. Research the types of jobs you might want online and pay careful attention to the words that are used in the job description itself. These are the terms and phrases you will want to use in updating your résumé.

3. Seek out a mentor, sponsor, or even a life coach. The benefits of having a mentor are great. Mentors help lessen much of the stress that comes from attempting to transition from military life into civilian life. Find someone who has been successful in transitioning into

civilian life, including into the civilian workforce.

4. Seek out military job and career fairs. Most major cities have career fairs just for military veterans in an attempt to alleviate the struggles of finding work. Similarly, there are recruiting firms, such as RecruitMilitary.com that specialize in placing military veterans into civilian jobs.

5. Network to find the resources you need in transition. Ask family and friends about connections they may have to the company with which you would like to be employed. Go to networking events, use social media, and even check local bulletin boards.

It can sometimes be incredibly difficult and frustrating to transition from military life to a civilian job. That is why it is very important to be prepared as best as one can. Creating a game plan is only part of the solution. You must also be willing to seek help from those close to you, as well as those that offer their resources through the government, non-profit organizations, and fellow veteran ran organizations and firms. Many times it is easy to convince oneself that doing it alone is just as easy, but during these difficult times, it is best to accept what help you can get, even if it is emotional support from a loved one. Obtaining help from those around you will make the transition much easier.

During your military career, did you ever have another Black woman as a mentor?

Yes, I had a wonderful mentor. Her name was CSM Patricia Williamson.

What was your experience like (or lack of experience) with a Black woman as a mentor?

I do not feel I would have made it to retirement without CSM Williamson. She took the time to tell me to stop looking at all the negative and start thinking positively about the military and my career. She said you are going to find this anywhere you go; it is in the civilian sector too. CSM told me there are great benefits here. Seek out those.

She asked me about my family, what I wanted to do in my career, and my goals. She then guided me on how to make it happen. She advised me on military schools and physical fitness and told me what it took to get promoted. I thank God for CSM Patricia Williamson. I know I could not have done it without her.

She wanted me to know there would be obstacles. but with God and faith I could get around them all. She retired years ago and we still stay in touch today. Her words truly helped me in my career and now I am eligible for MSG.

What would you tell other Black women who serve about taking on the role of a mentor to other Black women serving?

Please mentor another Sister as we all need to be pulled aside and encouraged along the way. Remember that what you make happen for someone else God will make happen for you.

My hope is that this book inspires my daughter who is also in the military and was recently on AGR (active duty Guard Reserve). She can retire in 9 years before the age of 40. She is a great leader and would serve as a great example for younger troops if she continues to serve.

Her challenge is that she is a mother with young children and it can be challenging serving in the military when you have small kids. I tell her the values she learns in the Army will be with her forever to teach them to her own children.

CAMOUFLAGED SISTERS

By wearing the uniform of the US Army for 23 years I have expressed my loyalty to my fellow Soldier as well as to the United States. I highly recommend you find a good mentor and seek her mentorship throughout your military career.

LEADERSHIP

"Leadership is about making others better as a result of your presence and making sure that impact lasts in your absence."

- Sheryl Sandberg, COO of Facebook

SDrRK98SMH

of December 15, 2016

Item

Camouflaged Sisters: Revealing Struggles of the Black Woman's Military Experience
Holley, Lila --- Paperback
1942838484
1942838484 9781942838487

3

Know Your Value

AMANDA RANDOLPH

We all come from different walks of life. Our backgrounds are different. Our heights, shapes, skin tones, and hair are different. Even the decade that we were born in may be different. But we do have several things in common. First and foremost, we have value. We have worth! Each of us is blessed with a unique set of gifts, skills and talents that can be used to help others learn and grow.

Another important factor we have in common is that we are classified ethnically as African American. Last but not least, we answered the call and chose to serve our great nation. We have experienced similar challenges, struggles, and successes in the profession we chose. We have learned what it means to be a leader and have success. We have also learned and experienced the kind of leader we did not want to be or become.

One other important commonality that cannot be overlooked or glossed over is that we serve or served in a profession dominated by males. According to the Department of Defense Demographic study published in 2012, females (Caucasian and African American) represented less than twenty percent of the active duty and reserve force in 2010, the year I retired from the Army. When I joined the army, twenty-six years earlier in 1984, approximately ten percent of the Active Duty force was female. This was reported in a Congressional Budget Office report on Social Representation in the U.S. Military published in 1989.

African American females are part of an elite pool of women with unique experiences we can all share, learn, and grow from. During my 26 years of Active Federal Service, most of what I learned about leadership was from the male leaders in the units to which I was assigned. From each of them I experienced what great leadership looks like and what the lack of leadership can do to one's morale. As a female military leader, you must recognize your own intrinsic worth and the value you bring to any unit or organization you are a part of.

Learning Leadership

In military circles, leadership is often defined or described as the art of influencing others to accomplish a mission. That in itself is not easily done. Many service men and women today want to know the "why" behind the "what." If they don't understand the "why" they may question the "what" you are directing them to do.

There are three leadership styles taught to service personnel: directing, delegating, or participating. In more recent times, situational leadership determines which style is used. As a new recruit arriving at Basic Training, I was introduced to the directing style of leadership. New recruits needed daily direction to learn military protocol, drill and ceremony, and leadership. When I went through basic training in 1984, Drill Sergeants were always in your face. Drill Sergeants were not there to coddle you, but to transform you from a civilian to a Soldier.

Basic Training was the first place where I was introduced to a female Non-Commissioned Officer (NCO). She was the lone female Drill Sergeant in a company of eight platoons. She was loud, vulgar, and in your face. In the 80's, it was often expected that female Soldiers and leaders had to be rough, gruff, and offensive in order to be considered equal to their male counterparts. Many female recruits in my platoon thought that this behavior was the norm and emulated her leadership style. I, on the other hand, did not conform to that standard. Being loud, vulgar, and in your face was not and never has been my personality type, nor did it become my leadership style.

Upon arrival to my first duty station, as a young Private First Class (PFC), I realized that all of my immediate supervisors were male. My squad leader, platoon Sergeant, First Sergeant and commander were all men. Although there were many women in the unit, very few female leadership examples existed. From 1958 until 1985, a parallel rank structure of non-commissioned officers (NCOs) and Specialists existed to differentiate between leaders and non-leaders. Non-commissioned officer ranks existed for those in leadership positions such as squad leader, platoon sergeant, and first sergeant, and the specialist rank existed for those not in leadership.

Not long after reporting to my duty section, my immediate supervisor asked me how I obtained the rank of PFC so quickly. What was unknown to him was that while in high school I served three years in the Air Force Junior Reserve Officer Training Corps program. Through this program I learned the basics of leadership and was able to enlist with a rank above my peers. My immediate supervisor made it a point for me and another male Soldier to compete against each other for future promotions.

When I realized this, I became frustrated, disheartened, and very insecure. I struggled to find my way, and it seemed every bit of progress I made was met with stumbling blocks and hindrances. One of the lessons I learned from this experience was never to foster negative unhealthy competition with those whom you are in charge of. Instead, fuel their passion for learning and growing to become better at what they do. Dr. Myles Munroe said it this way: "The purpose of true leadership is not to maintain followers but to produce leaders." This statement counters the maxim "In order to be a great leader, you must first be a great follower." I was always a follower until I discovered that there was a leader in me.

Catalyst ... Motivation

I continued to struggle with insecurity even as I progressed through the ranks. This insecurity held me captive. Why? There were many times during various assignments when others said I did not have what it takes to become a leader. Whenever I accepted that falsehood, I sold myself short. I entered the Army as a PFC and progressed to Specialist and Sergeant in a relatively short period of time, but I stalled after that. I watched as my peers from earlier years and earlier assignments progressed to Staff Sergeant (SSG) years ahead of me. From 1984-1992, I only remember having three African American female NCOs in the units I was assigned to. The first, SSG Louise Hayes, was the Personnel Action NCO in my first assignment. Lou was a friend when I needed a friend and helped me make it through the assignment without wanting to give up. The second was Sergeant (SGT) Mildred Ford. The third was SSG Irene Sabine.

Of the three, Lou had the greatest impact on my life. Lou was both a friend and a mentor. She walked me through the process of navigating the male-dominated chain of command that existed in the unit. I admired how she gained the respect of her Soldiers by walking beside them and participating with them. She was a leader that never asked her Soldiers to do something she had not done or was not willing to do herself. She took the time to walk Soldiers through processes that would help them improve. As a leader she always sought to develop the leadership potential in others. The lessons I learned from Lou helped me become the leader I became.

There were others who helped in my development as a leader. One such person was the Order of Battle

Technician who was a Chief Warrant Officer Two. I remember specifically asking him what it took to become a Warrant officer and he told me, "You don't have enough time in the service, nor do you have what it takes." I was shocked, but walked away smiling. I decided right then and there to prove him wrong and begin to change my career path in the military. I was still insecure, but I had an objective. That objective was to prove naysayers wrong and prove to myself that I could do all things through Christ who gives me strength. I often quoted Philippians 4:13 and Matthew 19:26 to myself when I needed motivation.

Transformation

Transformation is not easy. When I made the decision to passionately pursue becoming a Warrant Officer, I experienced some opposition. Some of it was my own doing, especially since I was years behind my peer group. The first thing I did was work on my records for promotions. I then enrolled in school to get an associate's degree. Before then, I would sporadically take correspondence courses and a university class here and there. Now that the decision was made, my focus was set on obtaining the required degree. This took some time, but I successfully obtained the degree and subsequently became a Warrant Officer.

Even after becoming a Warrant Officer, I struggled with insecurities. People told me that my military records weren't as stellar compared to others and that the reason I succeeded was because of affirmative action. Yes, the military still uses affirmative action to assess women and other minority groups into certain positions. I didn't want to believe it and even said I did not accept it. But the thought always remained in the back of my mind: *Am I as knowledgeable as my peers?* I compared myself to others and thought I had to be just like them in order to be successful.

Transformation means changing the way you see things. Encouragement from other female Warrant Officers – one Caucasian, the other African-American, and one male Warrant Officer counterpart – helped me change my perception of myself. Each in their respective positions taught me to believe in myself, trust my independent analysis, confer with others, modify assessments, and stick to my guns. I watched how senior officers trusted them to make sound judgments and assessments and not be thrown off when others disagreed with them. When I became comfortable with who I was as an individual, I stopped comparing myself to others. I overcame this insecurity when I embraced my peers in the Warrant Officer Corps and remembered what the transition from enlisted to Warrant Officer was like for me. Remembering helped me to seek out others and help develop the leader in them. Leadership can be lonely, especially when you are looking for others who look exactly like you but can't really find them. What do you do in those moments? Seek out senior leaders who will take the time to willingly impart their wisdom to you. If you can't find someone willing to do so, then invest in yourself.

Transformation means Challenge, *not* Competition. The adage "if you're the smartest person in the room, then you're in the wrong room" is true. Don't expect to grow if you don't challenge yourself or find others willing to challenge you. A scripture that reminds me of this is Proverbs 27:17, which states, "As iron sharpens iron, so a man sharpens the countenance of his friend." Iron cannot be sharpened without friction. Neither can our minds or skill sets be sharpened without challenge and healthy competition. Early on I learned what unhealthy competition looked like, so I always chose to present problems or challenges to my Soldiers that I knew they had the answer to. Several of my peers remarked I must have been a real good softball player because I always threw softballs to the Soldiers. My aim was not to play softball, but to build up their self-esteem by drawing on the knowledge that existed inside each of them. Make that one of your aims as well. Draw on the knowledge and capabilities of your subordinates and watch them develop into great leaders.

Don't be afraid to be you! Be the best you and leader that you can be. Use your gifts, talents, and skillsets to help develop the next generation of leaders. God Bless!

During your military career, did you ever have another Black woman as a mentor?

Yes, I actually had two. One was Staff Sergeant Louise (Lou) Hayes and the other was Specialist Four Jeanette Collins. Both of these women affected my life in different yet significant ways.

What was your experience like (or lack of experience) with a Black woman as a mentor?

My first assignment was to Army Security Agency, Camp Humphreys, Korea. I was 18 years old, fresh out of high school and on my first assignment thousands of miles away from home. I needed a friend and Lou became that friend. As I reflect back on the relationship, I now realize Lou was more than a friend, she was definitely a mentor. Lou took the time to show me how to navigate the unit, the Army, and how to keep my nose clean. When I wasn't sure of myself or thought I was going to fail, Lou encouraged me to let me know I had what it took to make the Army a career. Jeanette, on the other hand, introduced me to Christ and helped me to understand that through Christ nothing is impossible. These two phenomenal women showed me how to help mentor others.

What would you tell other Black women who serve about taking on the role of a mentor to other Black women serving?

Whether you think you are or are not a leader or can/cannot mentor someone else is irrelevant. People are observing you- your actions, attitudes, behavior, conduct, and your character. Someone is always looking for someone to show them the way. Be the best example that you can be for others to model. I must warn you – choose wisely those whom you will mentor. Be very discerning of those whom you mentor. Not everyone will seek you out for the good that you can impart to them; but for information that can be used as leverage.

Should you look for a mentor? I say yes, especially if you are ready to learn and grow. Look for someone who is smarter than you, has more experience than you, and is willing to share what she has learned over the years. I must warn you as well. Not everyone will have your best interest at heart and be glad to see you grow and learn and in some instances surpass her. You also must be discerning and choose wisely.

4

Remaining Professional and Poised During Your Toughest Challenges

PATRICIA WATTS

Being a leader in life certainly bears great significance, but to embrace that responsibility within the parameters of military life requires an entirely different level of responsibility and challenge, albeit not without the proverbial rewards. Leadership is not a right but a privilege, and it must be honed not with the ill-tempered tools of ego and arrogance, but with the lasting effects of purpose and meaning.

I joined the Army at 18. Initially, I suppose one could say it was in defiance with respect to my dad. I got pregnant and had a baby at 17 and fully intended to attend Howard University. Yes, I had my limitations at the time, but I was not above defying them. My father, on the other hand, was making other choices for me that he no doubt felt were in my best interest at the time. I am sure it was his way of demonstrating his love to me. However, I was 18 and fully aware that I was always right. That attitude comes with the territory of being on the threshold of adulthood, where one believes she is always right but is still somewhat fearful of taking that first step across the threshold into adulthood. And if I didn't want to follow my dad's lead, then it was my move. That first step proved to be quite a doozy!

As a diversionary tactic to escape his choices based on what suited him, not me, I found myself in basic training in the Army for six months, and within four months was given my first assignment in Berlin. It was 1985. That would be the beginning of my 22-year career in the military.

I was grateful that my mother was on hand to take care of my daughter during my absence. It was a mixed blessing. The constant moving and deployments associated with life in the military can be extremely hard on kids and, obviously, on parents. My mother and father were there to ensure a stable upbringing for my daughter that I could never have provided on my own. I am now the proud mother of a grown woman who has found her place in life, both professionally and personally.

As a woman of faith, I believe God puts us through certain situations and experiences so that we are prepared for something that calls us to grip the horns of courage and tenacity in situations that demand more of us than we ever thought we had. We have to learn to disassociate from fear, trust our instincts, and courageously move forward when at times our feet seem paralyzed. Throughout my years of service, I completed numerous assignments worldwide. One of my final assignments was in 2001, shortly after the horrific events of 9/11. I was in Omaha, Nebraska, working in counter proliferation and heading toward the finish line of my military career.

Then came the hiccup. It was the stumbling block thrown onto my path that initially felt like an obstacle but later revealed itself as a significant stepping stone. I was given one last assignment. I was ordered to go to Heidelberg, Germany, and within one month of arriving there, I was told to go to Italy to prepare for deployment to Afghanistan. This was my first deployment that took me to the heart of the combat zone. I had no familiarity with the troops over there for which I was responsible. I had 177 troops placed all over Afghanistan. The level of accountability that fell upon my shoulders was significant. There were but two objectives on my mind at the time: Successfully complete the mission and bring everyone back home.

Easier said than done.

A month later, a U.S. aircraft went down, and while none of my direct Soldiers were on board, 18 within our command were killed. As a Sergeant Major, it was my duty to go to the flight line and give my respects as the remains of those killed were boarded onto the aircraft for their final journey home. Eighteen killed. Gone, but not forgotten. Eighteen bodies making their final trek home. It's an experience that invades every cell in your body. It creates an indelible memory that initially invites trauma, despair, and feelings of hopelessness but later commands respect for the lives that were selflessly given in the name of freedom.

Needless to say, my morale did not just decrease because of that experience; it all but vaporized. Whatever range of feelings we did have become obsolete; we were all running on fumes. This experience had been an assault on our emotions, and it seemed as if nothing could assuage the mounting grief that took shape in many forms. As a leader, however, I understood that to dwell on the situation would allow for complacency to permeate the troops. I still had young men and women to lead. This was the military. This was a war zone. Accidents happen. This is a place where lives are in constant danger. Death should not come as a surprise, even though it always knocks us off our feet when it does.

To combat the potential of unattended complacency, I switched gears and embraced a desire that was placed upon my heart. I initiated a humanitarian service that would give us the opportunity to go into the local villages, including the orphanages and schools, to deliver care packages. Of course, certain protocols had to be completed in order to receive final approval, but I knew it was the right thing to do. When pen and paper, I wrote countless letters to organizations back in the U.S., hoping to appeal to their hearts of compassion, and asked if they could donate supplies on behalf of this heartfelt and selfless mission.

Ask and you shall receive. We quickly had two vans filled with various goods to give to the villagers. This was the inaugural delivery of what was to become a weekly purpose. Every Saturday morning we would visit the people in these villages and give them these care packages. The fact that we were still fighting the Taliban did not marginalize our efforts to spread a greater good, delivering not only much-needed supplies but also providing compassion, kindness and the human touch. From this endeavor, despite the ensuing battles that raged on around us, kindness trumped evil. Its effects were so infectious that by the end of our year-long commitment to this project, officers enthusiastically became involved alongside the J2 Soldiers.

Kindness does not discriminate with respect to rank. I believe it is a natural instinct for everyone. We just need the motivation to inspire it. Turning a negative situation into a positive one is not being naïve. It is the essence of leadership, and if I am given the opportunity to make others feel better and improve themselves with my presence, I must also strive to make an impact in my absence. It is through this particular project that I feel I was given the power to empower others, and at the same time, I was willing to join them in the opportunity to make a difference.

While I never had any direct casualties during my service, I did experience a significant number of incidents that challenged my faith and temporarily rocked my confidence, not only in myself but also in mankind in general. Yes, as I mentioned previously, God does prepare us for certain situations in life and will never give us more than we can handle, but that still doesn't mean that fear and anxiety are not present. In many cases, they ride shotgun and often try to assume control of the wheel.

But certainly not on my watch, right?

At one time, I had five females in my command who were sexually assaulted and raped inside the wire. One particular incident that greatly affected me involved a young female Soldier in her 20s who truly was a ray of sunshine to everyone she met. She was in charge of issuing badges to everyone coming into Bagram Airfield in Afghanistan. It was evident that everyone adored her. She was friendly, engaging and respectful. She was also confident, ambitious and determined. A natural athlete, she excelled in running and was known to knock out six- to seven-minute miles with the ease of a gazelle. Early each morning, she would go for a run inside the wire on the base. It was a routine to which she was devoted, clearly for physical reasons, but I am pretty sure it also protected her emotional and mental states.

One particular morning, without missing a beat, she began her pre-dawn run. I am sure she did this without thinking how this particular run would alter the course of her life in the blink of an eye. But it did. Upon exiting a porta-potty, she was grabbed by two men armed with weapons. As they reached for their bayonets, they chillingly warned her, "If you say anything, we will slice you up." They pulled her into a nearby bunker with a cement overhead that was concealed from primary view and proceeded to rape her. She blacked out, whereupon the assailants left her, all but for dead.

Since the young woman's strict attention to punctuality was well known, concern began to grow to nerve-wracking levels when she first did not show up for work at 7:30 a.m. and was still nowhere to be found three hours later. The MPs began looking for her and by mid-afternoon, they found her in the bunker and took her to the ER. During her stay in the hospital, the young lady emphatically refused any attention from male medical personnel and would not speak or eat for several days. Suicide watch was in full effect at that point. Her days were spent surrounded by those who cared about her while she just rocked back and forth and cried. It was like a knife to the heart for my troops to observe this situation.

The young lady eventually left for home but later wrote a letter to me explaining that a family member had raped her twice in the past. She assumed the guilt for the incident, and that burden left her in a state of emotional chaos for quite some time. It's easy to become emotional when things like this occur. Hatred can rear its ugly head, but as a leader, I had to take another road. I was responsible for being there for those who were dealing with depression and who were separated from loved ones, yet still commissioned with the responsibility of a mission. Although I worked 14-16 hours a day, I truly was on call 24/7. My door was open and continually revolving. I've seen things that cannot be unseen. I've heard things that should not fall upon one's ears; I've been the unexpected audience to grown men who have been reduced to tears. I have also been there for them, as I have learned that people truly need love.

The key to leadership is to understand people and to motivate them. A leader has to meet the needs of people to get them to do what needs to be done. And as I mentioned previously, I hope the ripple effect of my efforts can still be felt in my absence. I know the impact my troops made upon me has left footprints on my heart.

I am honored to have been given the privilege of being a military leader. I am blessed to take those experiences and make positive changes in my life and in the lives of others as I embrace a civilian existence that has not forgotten its military roots. In fact, it continually honors them. And that is a message that is far better lived than simply remembered.

During your military career, did you ever have another Black woman as a mentor?

I entered in the U.S. Army four months after graduating from high school, and my first duty assignment was considered elite since I was assigned to Berlin, Germany in 1986. We were surrounded by communism and I didn't have a clue what the U.S. Army was about or what my mission entailed. I was assigned to the Adjutant General's Office in which I was responsible for administrative duties. My Sergeant Major was a Black woman who taught me a lot as it pertained to doing my best, completing the mission, and maintaining a professional bearing while on duty.

What was your experience like (or lack of experience) with a Black woman as a mentor?

Unfortunately, After Sergeant Major Jones, I didn't have any other Black women mentors. Sometimes you need to be able to talk to those who have experienced certain things in the military because of their race and gender to be able to talk with. Sergeant Major Edith Jones was more than a mentor to me. She taught me what it was to be a respectful woman. She genuinely cared for people, and it was important to her to see our success. This was my first time away from home on foreign soil surrounded by men. I believe her direct mentorship was critical and led to my overall success.

What would you tell other Black women who serve about taking on the role of a mentor to other Black women serving?

I think as women we don't do enough with mentoring other women. Senior male officers have always done this and continue to. We have a responsibility to lead and train others. We also have a responsibility to ensure we create opportunities to empower others. It would be great if we let our guards down and began to trust one another as women. This is an area that, even today, we as women lack, but we should take an active role to reach out and help one another.

5

Persevering When Your Integrity is Questioned

CATRENA FINDLEY

For nine and a half years, I served the United States with pride, honor, and integrity as a noncommissioned officer and commissioned officer. I was now in the most challenging role of my military career. This position was also the most rewarding. The Army had opened the first Warrior Transition Brigade (WTB) at Walter Reed Army Medical Center, and I was selected as one of 40 nurses who would stand up the new organization as a nurse case manager (NCM). Near the end of my two and a half years with the unit, I had established myself as a force. I had a reputation for being organized, resourceful and highly efficient. Our mission was to ensure that each patient assigned received the best, cost efficient, timely care recommended by the medical providers, and that the patients be managed through the process in a timely manner. I was number one in my company at accomplishing this task.

That first year I was in the unit I transitioned 27 Soldiers either through the medical evaluation board, back to active duty, or on to civilian lives, even though I spent only nine months working due to my pre-term labor. This earned me the respect and trust of my patients, my peers, subordinates, supervisors, and providers. This was a tough job, but it was fun. We worked ten to twelve hours per day, five days per week, and half a day on Saturdays or Sundays. To this day, I have never worked as hard as I did for this unit, and I have never enjoyed being an Army nurse as much.

I didn't begin to hit burnout until my new supervisor arrived and threatened all that I had worked so hard to build. Within five days of taking over as my new supervisor, she had managed to challenge my integrity, break my faith and make me question if I should even remain in the military.

It was during my second year at Walter Reed, while working on a medical-surgical ward, that I was selected to transfer to the newly forming WTB. I came over to the unit as a Second Lieutenant promotable with roughly 20 months experience as a registered nurse. There I was, just honing my skills as a new nurse when I was suddenly selected to serve in an entirely different role. I had no idea what a nurse case manager was or what he or she did. Many of my peers were inquiring about going to the new unit, some with experience in the role. All I knew was that it was a new challenge and I was ready for it.

I began preparing for my new role by reading up on nurse case management training, practice, and certifications. It had been my experience that professional nurses seek national certifications. Just before my transition date, I went into preterm labor and was placed on bed rest for several months. I immediately began to fear the chances of survival for my baby. I struggled with my situation and my faith. I later delivered a son at 23 weeks 4 days. He weighed 1 pound 10 ounces. Today, he is perfect. Though I was in fear of losing my new position due to my current situation, when I received a visit from Brigade Senior Nurse Case Manager, I was later reassured that the position was still mine. She assured me that the unit was behind me and waiting to meet me. It was my introduction to the unit and the beginning of a wonderful relationship with other military professionals.

After the birth of my son and convalescence leave, I arrived at the new unit to meet my team and began my new role. Though initially I felt ill prepared for this new role, meeting the team would increase those fears. I was the most junior nurse in rank and years of experience. The other NCM(s) were Lieutenant Colonels, Majors, and a few Captains. I was immediately intimidated. Again, my faith was tested. I feared that God had taken me somewhere he hadn't prepared me for. I began to feel that my selection was an experiment, or perhaps my prior service experience had swayed the decision to select me. Or maybe I was being set up to fail. Either way, I knew I had big shoes to fill and still I was up for the challenge.

As I began to orient to the new unit, I realized that because this was a one-of-a-kind, newly formed unit I wasn't alone in my feelings. We were all novices in this role. Once I realized that, I dug deep into learning my job and taking care of Soldiers. I quickly gained a knack for case management and transitioning wounded warriors through the process. I superbly managed the care of the 20 wounded warriors assigned to me and often took on additional cases during leave cycles of other nurses. The role required long hours to care for the 20 or so high acuity wounded warriors and it required autonomy to get the job done. My supervisor afforded us that autonomy. I set my schedule to meet the needs of the patients. Monday through Wednesday, Thursdays were administrative or personal days and Fridays were make-up days.

Our challenges were getting the patients to their appointments and I developed a process of completing a calendar for each patient during his or her visit with NCM. The patient would sign, I would sign, and the squad leader would sign, and a copy went into the patient's records. This process dropped the no-show rate of my patient load to 2% when the Brigade as a whole was at 30%. I shared my process with other NCM in my company, and they adopted it as well. By the end of my first year in the role, I was no longer a novice, but a very comfortable intermediate NCM. I was selected by senior leadership as the NCM who briefed the incoming hospital staff on the role of the NCM in the WTB and as the behavioral health NCM, responsible for reporting patient status to all NCM(s) in the Brigade. My evaluation was outstanding, and I was on fire for the Army and nursing.

Halfway through my second year at the unit, I had settled into my role and appreciation for the position. My then supervisor was preparing for retirement, and a new supervisor came on board. My new supervisor came with no experience and with her own ideas of what this unit did. As my retiring supervisor prepared to depart the unit he shared with me the new supervisor's view on my situation as a NCM and a single parent and her differing view on how I was to accomplish my mission. His advice to me was to sit down with her for an initial counseling sooner rather than later. That was exactly what I did.

I got on her calendar. I requested to meet with her for an initial counseling that week. She was a little taken back by it, but I trusted it was the right thing to do. If I needed to reset my battle rhythm to meet her requirements I'd rather know sooner than later. Plus, I needed to inform her of my family situation. We met and I explained to her my process of managing my caseloads. I shared with her my schedule and that I keep a calendar on my door with my schedule and appointments. I also shared with her that I was a new divorcee with four children, one of which had developmental delay, and that I scheduled his appointments on Thursdays when I didn't see patients. Although I didn't get much feedback from my new supervisor, I felt the meeting went well. I went back to my office, shared my outlook calendar with my new supervisor and continued on with the status quo.

Three days later on a Thursday, I had an appointment for my son because I had no patients scheduled since I never scheduled patients on Thursdays. I learned a week later that a wounded warrior came by my office and sat and waited on me. She didn't attempt to reach me by cell, but instead began to discuss personal things openly in the open office, which caused the administrative assistant to seek someone to assist her. The patient was taken to my new supervisor and told my supervisor she was supposed to meet me that day. My supervisor checked the computer system and noticed I had 25 uncharted notes and concluded that I was overwhelmed with my caseload and reassigned that patient to another NCM. I didn't find out until a week later when I saw the patient and asked her to come see me to get her new schedule of appointments. The patient informed me that she was no longer my client. When I went to address this with my supervisor, she began to tell me that I was overwhelmed, and that she wanted me to seek behavioral health services. She told me that I would find myself hospitalized if I continued this way. I began to cry, but not tears of sadness – tears of anger. I said out loud, "that devil is a lie!" I asked her, "You've known me for five days; how do you know what I look like stressed?" She began to tell me that when her husband returned from Iraq as an alcoholic she had to get a nannie to survive, and there was no way I could be making it in this position as a single parent. I then told her that was the cloth she was made from, not me. Despite being a single parent I have never missed an appointment. I told her I was disappointed in her actions and informed her that I would be speaking with the senior supervisor.

That night I discussed the situation with my boyfriend, and he advised me to ask to be moved from under her supervision because trust had been broken and it was, at this point, irreparable. I was torn because I didn't want to leave my patients and believed things could be fixed.

The next day, I was emotionally exhausted. We both met with the senior supervisor and I began to tell my side of the situation. I inquired about the whereabouts of my professional courtesy, and asked why didn't someone call me or simply ask the patient or squad leader for that patient's calendar signed by all parties. My supervisor interrupted me to say she found 25 uncharted notes on my patients. I never denied the uncharted notes; however, the senior supervisor was already aware of why I had 25 uncharted notes and interrupted the conversation. She said to my new supervisor, "You are wrong and I need you to fix this. This 1LT has done outstanding things for this unit. She continues to perform above and beyond expectations. During a time of shortages just before your arrival, she carried a double caseload for six consecutive months without incidence, which is outstanding, considering the acuity of her patients. She is an excellent NCM and our unit would not have survived without her. Now, can we please move forward and past this?" The new supervisor answered yes and I agreed, since I did not want to leave my patients. I immediately felt vindicated and in my heart I wanted to believe we could move forward.

Later, the new supervisor began to systematically work to prove I was incompetent. She began trying to remove my extra duties and decrease my caseload. When I found out, I addressed this with the senior and requested to be removed from the section. The senior refused to move the new supervisor or me. I felt angry and failed by my leadership. I decided at ten years active duty service to resign my commission and leave the Army. It took a while but I got orders to leave the Army. Once the new supervisor realized I was leaving the Army, she let up on me. She even wrote a letter of recommendation for me to join the Uniform Public Health Service. It wasn't until my boyfriend at the time (now husband) told me to "never let someone who doesn't matter to you have power over your future" that realized I was giving her the power. I decided to resend my orders and continue on active duty.

I received my first Meritorious Service Medal (MSM) when I left that unit. It wasn't until after I left that I realized that this new supervisor still wasn't done. She decided to give me a less than stellar evaluation as I departed the unit. I tried to fight the evaluation that didn't match my previous evaluations or the MSM I received and didn't reflect my accomplishments in the unit. In the end, I spoke with the Brigade Commander who was now my senior rater, and he gave me an outstanding senior rater evaluation. He said to me, "I cannot influence her evaluation of you, but this supervisor also has to get an evaluation by me." I almost got upset about the evaluation. I felt defeated again. After two and a half years of successful performance in this very challenging role and two outstanding evaluations as a 1LT, I had worked too hard to have my first Captain's evaluation to be less than stellar.

Then I remembered this: God wants you to know He is all you need and that promotion comes from Him and not from man. When we forget that God is all we need. He will allow you to repeat the lesson. Just like all the other challenges I've faced, I persevered because God wanted me to. When faced with challenging situations or storms of life, you have to remember that God is all you have and He is all you need. His grace is sufficient.

During your military career, did you ever have another Black woman as a mentor?

No, I have never had a Black woman as a mentor.

What was your experience like (or lack of experience) with a Black woman as a mentor?

For the vast majority of my career I have found that there were very few Black female officers. Initially, I sought a mentor at all cost and it didn't matter their race; I just wanted a mentor. As a young Lieutenant I spoke with senior leaders about obtaining a mentor. My senior would push me toward other senior nurses who would not really accept my request for mentorship. I remember wanting direction and expressing my frustration with a White male Major who said, "LT, the leaders have chosen their mentees and they look just like them." It took me a minute to understand what he was saying. The leaders were White and the ones being mentored were also White. Though I didn't want to believe him, this would prove to be true throughout my career.

The one time I came close to a Black female officer to request a mentorship relationship, she began doing things to let me know she wasn't in my corner. She would go out of her way to correct .me, even if I wasn't wrong. I would find nuggets of beneficial information that she had shared with my White peers but failed to share it with me. I later addressed her with my issues with our relationship. I reminded her that when I met her she said if I need anything I shouldn't hesitate to let her know. I told her how excited I was to finally have a Black female mentor who could give me direction and help me understand the walk we have as Black females. However, she began to treat me as though I weren't as stellar an officer as my White peers. It was like she wanted to prove that she could be hard on Black nurses to avoid impartiality. I told her that I needed her guidance and knowledge to be successful.

What would you tell other Black women who serve about taking on the role of a mentor to other Black women serving?

I would say it is your responsibility to share your knowledge with the generations coming behind you. If you remember what it was like to be ill prepared for an assignment or a situation, then you know you have the capability to change that situation for other Black females in the military. We are a shrinking minority, and we will continue to shrink if we don't mentor our young.

BALANCE

"I am a woman in process. I'm just trying like everyone else. I try to take every conflict, every experience, and learn from it. Life is never dull."

- Oprah Winfrey

6

Keeping Your Family and Career Balanced

SYLVIA McCREA

In 2006, after being deployed to Iraq for eight months, I had to return home to deal with a medical issue that had worsened during my deployment. Doctors quickly determined that surgery was the best recourse. Unfortunately, there were setbacks during the recovery, which prolonged the recovery phase. Because of this, my supervisors decided that I would not rejoin the unit and Soldiers in Iraq. Upon telling my family, my daughter's response was, "Mommy, who's going to take care of your Soldiers?" I was very surprised by my daughter's comment and have often revisited that moment in my attempt to truly understand what it all meant. As I think back on those words today, eight years later, I can't say that I completely understand, but I have a good idea of what it all meant.

Initially I thought, oh, how sweet, my daughter understands how important my job is and how much

I care for my Soldiers. Then there were times when I thought, 'what kind of mother am I that my child would be so inclined to see taking care of my Soldiers as more important than being with her? I often asked myself, have I led my family to believe that my job was more important than them? Of course, I never asked my daughter or the rest of my family that question, because I was too scared of the truth. The point is, being a Soldier, a wife, and a mother had its challenges. The biggest challenge for me was trying to balance all three. To be honest, I don't believe I did a very good job balancing these three roles in my life, mainly because I was too busy trying to prove myself to my leaders, my peers, and my subordinates. Sadly, I gave way too much of myself to my job and being a Soldier to the point where I had nothing left to give when I got home.

Don't get me wrong, I love my family and they love me, and I took advantage of their love. I kept telling myself that I was doing it all for them; truth be told, I was doing it all for the approval of others. Furthermore, while I thought I had to prove myself to everyone, I was the hardest person to prove myself to, It didn't matter how many awards, pats on the back, promotions, or accolades I received; I still felt I needed to do more to prove that I was good at my job.

Now, that's not to say that there weren't those who really needed convincing. In fact, throughout my career, there were several individuals to whom I really had to prove myself. These individuals were mostly White male and senior ranking. I'm sure this doesn't surprise anyone since the Army is predominantly White male, particularly in the upper ranks. However, what surprised me is that the more senior I became the more I had to prove myself, and not only to my seniors, but sometimes even to my peers. Because of this, I felt I had to work harder and longer hours. I felt guilty when I had to take off to tend to my family or when I had to leave work early to fulfill a promise I made to my kids. I would overlook medical issues or injuries to make sure I was at work, "setting the standards" or better yet, proving myself. As a matter of fact, that is exactly why I ended up in Iraq with a medical condition, as I discussed earlier. I had known of my condition before I left. I knew there was a chance it would get worse, but I refused to complain about it, so I just overlooked it.

The balancing act, as I said, was a difficult task, and it still is, but I think it was one of the most important things I had to learn to do. I learned by thinking of life as a plate. Every aspect of my life was on that plate, and I had to make sure to balance that plate so that nothing important falls off, important being the key word. I had to decide that what was on my plate was not going to fall off, which of course was my family and my faith. When I did, the balancing act became a little easier.

I must confess I wish I had figured it out a little sooner, but I do not regret joining the Army or ever deciding to remain in the Army after becoming a mother and wife. I learned so much. I grew mentally, intellectually, physically, and spiritually because of the experiences, both good and bad. I learned a lot from the people I served. Additionally, I learned a lot about myself — my positive attributes as well as my flaws. One of the good, and most important, things I learned is that I am a lot stronger than I thought. I used to think, before I even did anything, that I would fail. Because of the many accomplishments and challenges that I was able to meet in the Army, I now know that I am strong and capable of doing much more than I think I can. I now take on challenges that I never would have before. Because of what I've learned, I don't put everyone else's thoughts about me ahead of my own or the people I trust. I don't look for people's acceptance and approval. I know if I am doing my best, that's all anyone can ask for, even me.

I also learned that how I am is how God intended me to be. I was told on several occasions that I wasn't loud enough or assertive enough, especially by male peers and supervisors; but I learned that my compassionate, calm demeanor worked for me, and it didn't hinder me from getting the job done. Finally, and most important, I learned not to beat myself up when I made mistakes, even the mistakes I made as I learned to balance my roles as a mother, wife and Soldier. I learned to forgive myself and to learn from my mistakes.

During your military career, did you ever have another Black woman as a mentor?

I did not have a Black woman as a mentor. However, while in the Army, I met several Black women who taught me how to be a Black woman in the Army and how to deal with certain issues, such as racism and sexism. The first one that I recall was a Black Captain I met while serving in the U.S. Army Reserves. She wasn't with my unit, and I only spent a week with her. I never saw or heard from her again; however, I remember her getting on me after I had presented myself in an unladylike manner. She first scolded me and said, "I know your mama didn't raise you to talk like that." She was right. She then pulled me aside and told me to never act like everyone else just to fit in. I never forgot that lady or what she said to me that day.

Again, although I didn't have a Black woman mentor me, I learned from other Black female Soldiers. I learned by observing them and listening to them. I learned how to carry myself, how to project my ideas, how to be positive, how to protect myself, and how to be the best at whatever I did. I also learned from them how to deal with people, and how not to deal with people.

What was your experience like (or lack of experience) with a Black woman as a mentor?

I believe because I didn't have a Black woman as a mentor, there was a lot I had to figure out on my own, and unfortunately, it was sometimes a slow process. When I ran into issues, especially of a racial or a gender matter, I didn't know who to call. Of course there were Black men and men and women of other ethnic backgrounds that I could talk to and solicit advice from, but it wasn't the same. Oftentimes, when seeking advice from someone other than a Black woman, either I was misunderstood (being too sensitive, not taken seriously, etc.), or it would turnout that the advice was not good or appropriate.

It was definitely a challenge, but it made me stronger and more definitive in my approach to situations. I learned to use what worked for me.

Excuse my redundancy, but I want to reiterate that most of my learning came through my Black women peers and friends. Peers and friends like Lila Holley and others whom I learned from by observing their actions, listening to their stories, and sharing in their experiences.

What would you tell other Black women who serve about taking on the role of a mentor to other Black women serving?

I would tell them that it is a very important role, not only in the military setting, but also in the civilian setting. Since we're focusing on the military setting, I will limit my remarks to that area. Since my daughter is in the Army, this issue hits very close to home for me. When it comes to Black women not mentoring young Black women, I think it's either they do not know how important it is for young Black women to have a Black woman mentoring them, or they have perceive, just like in the civilian sector, that young Black women don't want a mentor. My message to Black women who have been in the military for some years is to search out one or several Black women to mentor or start a mentorship program, because whether you know it or not, it is very much needed and they want it. Even if they can mentor one young woman, it would make a difference for that one. How awesome it would be for that one to have someone that understands what she's going through and how she feels. Going back to my daughter, although I do what I can in mentoring her as a young Black woman in the military and she appreciates it, I'm sure she would appreciate it even more if she had a mentor close by.

7

Overcoming Male-Dominance & Chaotic Situations

SINCERIA ALLEN

I can't believe it. What did I just do? You have just decided to join the United States Army at the age of 19. Are you crazy? Yep, you just gone and done it now, kid! What were you thinking was going to happen to you now? You have just joined the Army, which is mostly dominated by men. Well, it is too late to turn back now. You are on your way to basic training at Fort Leonard Wood, Missouri - better known as Fort Lost in the Wood.

I arrived at Ft. Leonard Wood the first week of August 1992. Early in the morning I was placed on a cattle bus with no idea what or where I was going to next. All I knew was my life was about to change forever. I know I had eight weeks to be here before I was going to be shipped off to Augusta, Georgia, to my

Advanced Individual Training to become a Signal Support Specialist.

All I kept replaying in my head as I was riding on the cattle bus to my new destination were the last words my uncle said to me in front of my dad in front of our house the day before I left out to the Military Entrance Processing Station to be shipped out to Ft. Leonard Wood for basic combat training. The last words that came out of my uncle's mouth were, "Your life will never be the same, kiddo; mark my words you will never be the same person again." He wished me the best of luck.

I did not know what to expect when I got off the cattle bus. Then, the cattle bus came to a complete stop and drill sergeants jumped on the bus yelling, "Get off the bus private! Welcome to my world!" I grabbed my duffle bag as I got off the cattle bus! All I could think was WHAT IN THE HELL DID I GET MYSELF INTO? My uncle and dad did not lie to me when they told me my life was never going to be the same again. The drill sergeants told us that we were one of the first all-female battalions at Ft. Leonard Wood. They welcomed us to the worst eight weeks of hell that would prepare us to be Soldiers in the U.S Army.

Boy, did I start to appreciate my parents after the first week in basic combat training. I realized that it was time for me to grow up. I had to learn quickly about how I was going to overcome the challenges of being in the Army as a minority and a woman in a male-dominated world. The Army was definitely not going to accommodate me. I had eight weeks to get physically fit and adapt to this competitive Army lifestyle. Being in the Army was truly a hard transition for me, especially since I had never been away from home more than two weeks by myself. I had to rethink how I was going to adapt to my new environment in this predominantly male environment.

After basic combat training, I was shipped out to Augusta, Georgia, to Ft. Gordon, home of the Signal Corps. I had 18 weeks to learn how to become a Signal Support Specialist. This was not going to be an easy task because there were definitely more men than women in this MOS. I remember telling myself, I am going to have to work harder and definitely know the ins and outs of this job if I expect to gain the respect of my male counterparts – these male Soldiers are not going to give me the same respect unless I earn it. As a Signal Support Specialist Soldier, I had to learn and develop technical skills necessary to transmit voice, automation, and digital data across all worldwide networks. I remember that we had only four females in my class of about thirty Soldiers. Out of the four females, only two were Black. Only three of the four female Soldiers graduated out of the Advanced Individual Training (AIT) graduated. However, I was the lucky one to be assigned to Fort Drum, New York, 10th Mountain Division after completing AIT. Ft. Drum was home to light infantry division, and not even male Soldiers wanted to go to Ft. Drum if they were not infantry Soldiers.

When I arrived in Ft. Drum in February 1993, I had to overcome the fear that my first duty assignment was in very cold upstate New York. The majority of this duty station was seventy-five percent infantry Soldiers. I remember that the biggest challenge at my first duty assignment was earning the respect of junior and senior leadership. I had to work on insuring my chain of command that I was able and willing to accomplish all my assigned tasks and missions given to me in the communication shop.

There was already a stereotype about female Soldiers established by the male Soldiers in this unit. They felt that the female Soldiers were not holding their weight in the unit. The male Soldiers felt that some of the female Soldiers had used too many excuses to get out of doing their MOS. I was in a maintenance forward support company. Our main mission was to work on all types of equipment that needed repair or replacement from the infantry battalion we supported. So a lot of time the male Soldiers made jokes about how the equipment was too heavy to lift if I could please move the radios out the back of the truck or take the battery out the truck. I definitely experienced a strong feeling of being unequal in the unit. I never let that get to me. though, and I learned how to be more resourceful. I used things in my work environment to help me maneuver around the vehicles as I worked on the signal communication systems. I learned if I tried to do things first by myself I would earn more respect from my male counterparts who worked with me in the maintenance bays. I found they were more willing to offer help and assistance with working on communication equipment. Still, I knew I had to earn their respect and break the stereotypes they believed about female Soldiers in the Army.

It was a cold spring day during which our unit was doing a field training exercise (FTX) for two weeks. Our battalion commander decided to have some fun with the FTX and have a little competition throughout the battalion. The competition was a survival of the fittest course. No information was given to any of the Soldiers, and we were all broken up into five to six Soldiers teams. Each team had a radio Soldier. I remember one of my male counterparts, a signal

Soldier, stating the team that had a female Soldier. He said their radio Soldier was not going to win because the female Soldiers were not physically fit enough to carry the radio across the survival course without having the male Soldiers help carry it. Well, I took that statement as a personal challenge without him even knowing – it was game on. Needless to say, our team was the first team to cross the survival course finish line without me even giving up the radio the whole time and keeping in step with my fellow male Soldiers. That was my first call out for being a female Signal Support Specialist Soldier; I knew there were going to be many more.

From that day forward, I knew I had to operate at a standard above my male counterparts. The way I kept ahead was to learn my job and make sure I understood the mission that had to be accomplished by my chain of command. I also knew that I had to know Army regulations if I wanted to advance through the ranks to become a junior and senior non-commission officer (NCO). I had to be able to do my job, which was to train and lead Soldiers that fell under me. I knew that sometimes I could be a hard leader, but I wanted the Soldiers to know their jobs because one day Sergeant Allen was not going to be there and I wanted them to be able to excel and accomplish the mission.

Another obstacle I had to overcome in my military career was being able to be a wife, mother, and Soldier in the Army. I discovered new challenges when I got married to another Soldier. The Army was not always accommodating to Soldiers married to each other and with children. I had to quickly learn the regulations on how the Army handled dual military spouses and children, because a lot of the chain of command was not supportive or did not understand how to deal with dual military families. The infantry chain of commands that were made up of all male leaders did not do well with handling a Soldier married to another Soldier with children. I remember one day when my ex-husband came home from work and told me his chain of command had never really dealt with dual military Soldiers before. His commander jokingly said, "If the Army wanted you to have a wife and children they, would have issued one." This little joke made being a woman, mother, wife and a minority in the Army even more challenging. I had to always remind myself to pray about it and look to God for answers because I definitely didn't know how I was going to carry on with all these different titles I now had. It was not easy being a wife, mother, and Soldier in the Army. The male counterparts didn't understand the problems of learning to manage all these different titles in their heads.

In the process of learning to manage all this, I learned to better manage my time wisely between the military, family, and marriage. Now, I had to be on top on my game at work as well as be a role model for my two daughters. I wanted my daughters to know that there were no limits in life, and that they could do whatever they wanted to do without being placed in a stereotype box. I wanted them to know that the sky was the limited and they shouldn't let people put them in a box. And I want you all to know this, too. Be confident in who you are, and know yourself; look to your inner beauty, and know who God is in you. I continually reminded myself that I am a queen in God's eyes, and that I could do all things with Christ Jesus within me. I realized that even during my hardest time in the military, God kept me close to him, and I thank Him for that. I knew God would not let me down. Just stay focused on the mission, make a plan, and make it simple for everyone to understand. Then, execute the plan.

My last chapter in the military was at Fort Hood, Texas. I came to Ft. Hood to work in the S6. Over the years, I learned a lot about how to build a stronger professional relationship with my chain of command, to always know what the mission is and what it takes to complete it, and to be a leader able to train and lead Soldiers at all times. I always remember to put

God first, then family and then my job – this has been the key to my success.

During your military career, did you ever have another Black woman as a mentor?

During my military career I was blessed to have had several encounters with Black female senior and junior non-commissioned officers (NCOs) in my unit in Germany. The Black female NCOs made sure that the junior enlisted understood that the Army was not an easy road to travel being a Black woman in a male-dominated Army. The Army regulations for the physical training (PT) weight requirement definitely were not in the favor of the Black woman, and we needed to work as teammates to encourage and motivate each other to strive to be the best and do our best. The Black female NCOs always tried to lead by example. Along with educating us about physical fitness, they valued giving advice on what area to work on when exercising in the gym and what to eat to ensure healthy eating habits. The Black female NCOs also worked with junior enlisted females by teaching us what to study when it was time for us to go to Soldier of the month boards, which assisted in preparing us for the promotion board.

What was your experience like (or lack of experience) with a Black woman as a mentor?

The greatest mentor I had during my whole military career was my battle buddy, SPC Livingston. She was just like the Bible states, "iron sharpening iron." She was the person who kept me accountable for the accomplishments, goals, and objectives that I needed to meet in order to get promoted in the Army. We worked together hand in hand, learning what education we needed to get for promotion points. We worked on pushing each other to accomplish great/good physical fitness scores on our PT test by working out at the gym together during lunchtime or after work. We kept each other abreast of what changes were being made with Army regulations along with helping each other better understand how to apply the regulations to our careers. We studied together to go to promotion boards as well as Soldier of the month boards. I am thankful to have had such an amazing strong Black woman in my life, who continues to help give me guidance during good times or bad times. She has always encouraged me to push myself further, and because of that I was able to what I might have given up on. We understood the other's personality, which allowed us to assist each other in moving up the ranks by promotion in the Army.

What would you tell other Black women who serve about taking on the role of a mentor to other Black women serving?

It was very tough to climb the staircases of success and get promoted in the military, which is dominated by men. The struggle was, and remains, real for Black women in the Army, and my recommendation is to keep your accomplishments, goals, and objectives in front of you at all times. Work on yourself and know your job descriptions, what requirements you need to get promoted, and how to perform your job. Ensure that you are able to give knowledge to the coworkers and Soldiers you lead.

A true leader is able to lead her Soldiers, but the best leader is a leader that teaches her Soldiers how to do their job while she remains confident. Helping other Black female Soldiers will help bless you. Knowledge is powerful, and that is what we need to pass on to our fellow Black women in the military.

8

Utilize Your Resources When Feeling Overwhelmed

KEISHA MOULTON

I can remember the hot days of basic military training like they happened yesterday. The San Antonio sun beat down on my BDUs. The sweat from my forehead dripped down into my eyes; it burned. I was only 18 years old. It was my first week of basic military training with the United States Air Force. At this young age, I had never felt more proud of myself as I did during this time. In the years to come, it would still remain one of the top 3 personal accomplishments. I am most proud of these! It was easy for me to make friends, given my naturally outgoing personality. It was harder to navigate through the various stages of training. My instructor insisted that she would break me of my attitude problem; I insisted that she wouldn't! What attitude problem? I'd often think to myself. I learned so many things about myself during my time as an active duty Airman. I somehow had to learn to put the needs of the mission before my own, my daughters, and all else. I can remember the countless days and nights that passed as I tried to adapt to my new way of life. Working tired, working sick, working overtime, and of course plain old working out.

Being Active Duty as a single mother, combined with being a Black woman, was difficult. There didn't seem to be any genuine outlets made readily available to me as a woman serving in the military. I believe this should have been different. Many times I wished I had somewhere to turn, or someone to talk to. My many sleepless nights as a young, single mother began to weigh heavily on me. Trying to carry the weight of this responsibility was tough. It was hard enough for some intact, two-parent active duty families to bear, let alone a single parent, active duty family. I would not have felt so isolated or alone at times if there perhaps had been a support group of people in similar situations for me to relate to.

One of the most challenging obstacles I faced was time management. My oldest daughter Michelle and I had a rigorous routine. Before I returned to work from convalescent leave after giving birth, we actually had a practice run of our typical day. I set my alarm and dressed my beautiful newborn, and then we set off.

We mocked the drive from my tiny apartment right outside of Lackland Air Force Base. We made our way to our new babysitter's home. She was actually the wife of one of my fellow Airman. It was an unconventional arrangement, to some. As it turns out, she was also staying home to care for their infant son. He had been born a few weeks before Michelle. But I was grateful for the help! As all military families can relate to, there is no such thing as "calling in to work" in the Armed Forces. I would not be given any room for error in reporting for duty. I used our practice run as a guide to a typical day — how early we would need to get up, leave the house, safely drop Michelle off, and arrive to work with plenty of time to spare.

Once I arrived to my duty section, I took my responsibilities as a Health Services Management Journeyman seriously. I gave my all to my supervisors, co-workers, and most importantly my patients, each and every day. I thoroughly enjoyed my duties and had a very high sense of pride in helping others. During my time in the service, I was called upon to multi-task more times than I care to remember. I must add that I do not believe in the term "multi-task'," specifically for Soldiers. I feel as though this word actually means to focus on one portion of a task while another portion of it lacks in some way. This is one of the reasons time management became so important to me. I began to break my day into segments, which was crucial since I worked 12-hour shifts. I then did my best to focus on the remaining portion of my day. Typically, after I left base, I picked Michelle up from the sitter. After we got home, I fed her, bathed her, and got her ready for bed. Once Michelle was settled for the night, I tried to get at least a few hours of sleep. It sometimes seemed as though, just as I placed my head on my pillow, the alarm was sounding. Then before we knew it, the time had come for us to repeat our cycle once again.

There were many times I wished more of my fellow Airmen, as well as my NCOs, would have checked in on me. I wish they'd asked me questions such as, "How are you *really* doing? Is there anything I can do to help make your day easier? May I pick up Michelle for you today?" This is *not* to say I was completely neglected, by any means. I simply wish there had at least been additional outlets or support groups in an official capacity. When I look back on these trying times, it reminds me how we are a part of such an all-encompassing organization. As the Armed Forces, we have one common goal in mind: defending our nation. A large number of us are doing the exact same job in the exact same location or one like it, yet we still really never take time to get to know the very people we fundamentally entrust with our lives.

Even now, this is something I have made somewhat of a personal mantra in the civilian sector. I always try to take it upon myself to genuinely get to know people. I know it may sometimes feel as though you are alone and no one would understands what you are going through. Just always know that as a Service Member or Veteran you are not alone. There is always someone to hear your cry or answer the questions you have. Someone can help you sort through the issue you are facing right now. You just have to make the first step and reach out for help. Whatever it is you are facing, you do not have to face it alone! Sometimes I was left feeling as though I had nowhere to turn and no one who truly understood. This has always puzzled me. I think we need to work together to change it!

Fighting fatigue was another issue I found myself facing. As military women, we are expected to perform at high levels of stress. To me, it seems as though no one takes into account what stressors we might be simultaneously battling on the home front. At times we are often dealing with family issues, health issues, and financial issues, just to name a few. At the same token, we are often seen and upheld as heroes, Women of Steel if you will. Although, in being viewed as such, it can possibly make us feel either one of two ways: inadequate or like we need to overachieve and live up to that expectation. It is so necessary to make sure we take care of ourselves, not only as women, but as military women, perhaps *especially* as military women. So many complex things are demanded of us on a day-to-day basis. In order to even begin to tackle what is required of us, a healthy lifestyle is definitely necessary. Eating proper foods, sleeping well, exercising, and managing stress come to mind. These are all a part of maintaining a healthy lifestyle. You can seek help with these concerns through your Family Support Center and your Health and Wellness Centers (commonly called HAWC). It is important to take time to recharge and find ways to relax. A healthy, happy Soldier is more easily able to remain mission-prepared.

I know some days seemed longer and harder than others. It can seem as though your responsibility to our nation is overlapping into many, if not all, aspects of your day-to-day life. I have been there and can relate to your feelings of being overwhelmed. It is a huge responsibility we have, working each day to secure the freedom of those around us. At times, I am sure it can feel like a thankless job. This isn't true! Just know many people support what you are accomplish each and every day. The sacrifices you are making do not go unnoticed. You *are* appreciated. There are networks and support groups you can be matched with, depending on your immediate needs. You can receive help from the Air Force Aid Society if you are in need of such things as household goods, financial counseling, and assistance with a budget. If it is childcare you are seeking, each base has a program set up for this as well. They also offer a sliding scale, and will give a personalized rate for childcare service based on your income. It is amazing how receiving assistance through your duty station can alleviate some of the stress that comes along with selecting a trustworthy childcare provider.

If spiritual guidance is what you seek, there are specially trained chaplains available for you and your family. My base chaplain and his wife mentored me during one of my overseas tours. Having support from them during times of duress, as well as celebratory times, proved to be priceless. I continue to use some of the coping mechanisms and guidance given by them. Sometimes, I was seeking a sounding board for a personal issue. Other times, I needed to resolve a career-related matter. By simply allowing them to be helpful to me, many of my spiritual needs were addressed.

Continuing your educational goals is another great way for you to ensure your time in service will count toward a special certification or a degree you may be seeking. It is important to plan ahead for your educational goals. Also consider how your military career may line up with your career goals after you retire or separate from your branch of service. Do you plan to continue with your military profession in the civilian sector? Are you planning on taking an entirely different career path? These are just a couple of questions to ask. It is extremely important to take advantage of each benefit available to you as well as your family members. I know it can be hard to imagine fitting continuing education into your already packed daily schedule. However, it is definitely something to keep in mind as one of your benefits of continued service.

Throughout your career, there may be obstacles and trials you will find yourself facing. I know how this feels. You will overcome them. You are stronger and much more capable than you will ever know. If you remember to look within yourself, you are your greatest cheerleader. There are also many resources available to you, and the majority of these services will cost you nothing. Please do not hesitate to seek these resources if you need them. You are paying a debt with your service each day, which is irreplaceable. It is not one you, or anyone around you, takes lightly. It is one with which the world holds in high regard. On your darkest days, when it seems as though nothing else could go wrong, when it feels as though your load couldn't get any heavier, seek assistance and comfort. More often than not, this help will come from those who have been in similar situations. Do not feel alone. You are cared for, thought of, and, most importantly, prayed for more often than you will ever know! Press on Soldier, with your head held high and proud.

During your military career, did you ever have another Black woman as a mentor?

During my military career, my supervisor tried her best to mentor me. She had small children and her spouse was active duty. With so many time restraints, she was unable to juggle the amount of tasks she needed to accomplish in a given time. So I would have to say, no, it was not consistent enough to make a difference.

What was your experience like (or lack of experience) with a Black woman as a mentor?

Due to my lack of a mentor, I feel as though there were times I could have used additional guidance in making decisions directly related to my career. I could have also used a supportive voice for matters concerning my home life. I frequently found myself feeling as though my opinions went unheard.

What would you tell other Black women who serve about taking on the role of a mentor to other Black women serving?

If there are African American women looking to mentor a fellow service member, I would tell them to definitely go for it! They probably do not quite realize the positive impact this will have on the mentee. This, in turn, will make a positive impact for women in the service overall. Upon arrival to their duty stations, service members should have a list of Mentor Volunteers made available to them.

FAITH

"When you stand and share your story in an empowering way, your story will heal you and your story will heal someone else."

- Iyanla Vanzant

9

Be Unstoppable in the Face of Adversity

SHIRLEY LaTOUR

Have you ever imagined that you were in a different or better place, a different world even, a place where there are extremely early mornings and twilight nights, only to do it again and again, day after day? Have you ever left home not knowing exactly where you were going but are open and willing to explore what was ahead, so you ventured out ALONE? Have you ever written down a dream as a child or adult, and, years later, realized what you wrote actually did come to pass? Are you still dreaming? I am!

From start to finish, God has always been there for me, and He is there for you! My purpose for this chapter is to encourage you and to let you know that dreams do come true! It is possible to overcome your adversity and rise to the occasion.

Before the Move

Life at home during my childhood was not the best, although it was not as bad as some may have endured. There were many good days, but the bad ones tended to linger in my head. I am the fourth of six children. I had very low self-esteem and was self-conscious. These feelings were largely due to not feeling pretty. Other issues plagued our home. I wondered where I could go to be in a normal family.

The day came when an Army recruiter visited my high school. I had found a way out! I was 17, in my senior year and had to wait until graduation to leave for basic training. I had travelled many times up and down the East Coast with my family but never alone to an unknown place so when the day came, I was a bit scared. Mom was reluctant to let me go, but Dad was proud of my decision to join the Army; he is a Vietnam Veteran.

Barely 18 and a new high school honor graduate, 10 days after graduation, I was on my way to a new life. The recruiter drove me to Indianapolis, Indiana, from Fort Wayne, Indiana, where I boarded an airplane for the first time in my life, on my way to Fort Leonard Wood, Missouri. I had no idea what I was getting myself into!

SHIRLEY LaTOUR

The Awakening

Were cattle trucks made for transporting people too? I think not! The horror I felt as I was made to get on this cattle truck with other young people, strangers from all over the United States, is still fresh in my mind. I felt lost, but I was determined not to give up just yet. The recruiter said the Army would pay for college, and since I didn't know how that would be accomplished back home, I kept the hope and faith that I would make it through this new life adventure. Basic training: what can I say about it? Grueling challenging, many nights of tears, a lot of learning what life is really about, building trust and camaraderie amongst people of all races, ethnicities, and backgrounds from all over the world, and discipline.

I became friends with other young Black women who were just as lost as I was. We bonded in that short time and endured much together. By the time I graduated from basic training, I had matured greatly. My family was at my graduation and I was thankful for that, but then came another separation. I boarded a bus and headed to Fort Sam Houston, Texas for Advanced Individual Training (AIT). Along the way I discovered that life was much bigger and diverse than just Indiana. I had always been adventurous and willing to take on a challenge, even though I was quiet and reserved to those who didn't know me personally.

I had a dream of becoming a Registered Nurse since about the 7th grade. The recruiter knew this from day one and he told me they would send me to nursing school in AIT, which was a lie! You know the lies that are told to meet a recruiting quota, but no one else has experienced that, right? Combat Medic – that's what I was called when I reached AIT, even though it was doctored up to read Medical Specialist when I enlisted. I was terrified. What did that mean? I had initially joined the Army to leave home and go to college for "free." My young mind did not comprehend the possibility of "combat."

One of my drill sergeants was a Black woman, and I looked up to her even though at first I thought she was mean. It was her job to prepare us for what was to come and she did her job quite well. Right before graduation, she came in the barracks and into my bay. I thought I was in trouble! She had actually come to talk to me, not something a Drill Sergeant usually does with the troops. She told me she was hard on me because she could see my potential! It went a long way in my spirit and I am grateful! It was transition time once again.

SHIRLEY LaTOUR

Enlisted Life

From the time of enlistment in June 1997, I knew that my first duty assignment after training would be Korea, a WORLD away from family and friends that I had known. The fact that I already knew my next destination took a lot of the anxiety away. Life was grand in a foreign land! I met more diverse people and appreciated being away from home. While in Korea I became pregnant with my first child, so I returned to the United States after only 10 months and four days of service there. Oh how life had changed in a twinkle of an eye.

I faced many emotions during that time. I was alone, without the father of my baby, without my family in a place literally on the other side of the world. Confusion, guilt (I was raised in a holiness church), and depression set in. I didn't know what to do or where to turn. At one point I was even suicidal, not wanting to live because things fell apart in my world. I felt I had let God, my parents, and myself down. My battle buddies tried to help but they didn't know how. I never went to see anyone about my feelings, just God. He was the PERFECT one to talk to; after all, He made me! I remembered my upbringing in church, so I finally went to Him in prayer. I had rebelled and thought that because I was away from home I could do whatever I wanted. Yes, I could, but it all had consequences.

I was barely 19 when I had my son. Life was never going to be the same. I refused to go back home with a child and feel or be defeated. He was mine to love and provide for and that is what I did as a single mother at my next duty station, Fort Carson, Colorado. I was a single Black mother in the Army, and while there were challenges, there was nothing that couldn't be overcome with a strong mindset and support from others. For me, the moral support came from my church family in Colorado. Thank you Bountiful Blessings Church of God in Christ family!

I faced many ups and downs while at Ft. Carson, including two Article 15s and a demotion. I faced a White female Commander who was out to get me. I had sustained a knee injury while in basic training and suffered through it, not wanting to be seen as weak to my leaders and peers. After about two years of running through extreme knee pain while running the hills of Ft. Carson, I went to sick call for it. Long story short, I was given a permanent profile after all the testing was completed. My commander didn't like it and tried to have me discharged from the Army saying that I was not fit for duty. She went so far as to make me another appointment with my doctor, to which she came and tried to tell the doctor what to do as far as my profile. But God said otherwise! She then had me transferred to a new unit, which was no better. That Company Commander was a White man and was prejudiced against Black women. There were several of us in that unit, so we stuck together. Thankfully, while there, I was able to reenlist for Hawaii so I only stayed in that unit for only six months! I was determined not to give up. My mindset was that I had entered the Army voluntarily and would leave voluntarily! While in Colorado, I met my future husband. We wed on August 20, 2001 in Honolulu, Hawaii, when my son was two and a half, and we remain married today.

Hawaii was marvelous! Both the unit and our church family were very supportive. Approaching my 10th year in the Army at this point, I remembered the dream I had as a child of becoming a Registered Nurse and started back to school. More obstacles came to stop me but God again made my crooked paths straight! I was determined to do it; I had almost forgotten the initial purpose of joining the Army. But at the time, my eyes began to be opened. I had put my all into serving others, but I had neglected myself. I had learned many lessons in life and was ready to reach the goal and dream I had set out for myself. A Black female Sergeant First Class (SFC) by the name of SFC Goines-

Audrey came to my rescue! She mentored me through the process of putting in my packet to go to the AMEDD Enlisted Commissioning Program (AECP). Selected as a First Select into the program where I would go to nursing school full time, still drawing my Staff Sergeant pay and allowances, it was and still is one of the Army's best-kept-secrets!

In June 2008, my family and I moved to Fort Hood, Texas. where we still reside, and I began my second phase of nursing school. In December 2010, I graduated from the University of Mary Hardin-Baylor, Belton, Texas, with my Bachelors of Science in Nursing, in the top 10% of my class and was inducted into the Honor Society of Nursing. God has been faithful to me throughout the years! Yet another transition was about to unfold, and, looking back now, it is amazing how God works!

From Enlisted to Officer

March 2011 marked another milestone in my life, one I had never imagined as a Private E-1 when I first joined the service. I was commissioned as a Second Lieutenant in the Army Nurse Corps! Sometime in 2012, I was rummaging through some old things and came across my high school senior yearbook. I sat and looked through it, and to my surprise, I had already written my future in the book! I had forgotten what I wrote, but God knew all along, and He made it come true. See, I had written that I was going to become an Army Nurse! At present I sit here writing this as a Captain, an Army Nurse, a business owner, mother of two, married, and still in awe of God's wonder, grateful that He never gave up on me even when I felt unworthy of His love. I am still dreaming and still excited about the future 18 years into this Army journey! I am honored to serve my country and if I had to do again, I'd do it the same way!

You can do it, too! Whatever you set your mind to, you can achieve. So what, you had a few setbacks. Everyone has setbacks. The obstacles are out there, just jump over them! Some may not admit their mistakes, but those that do and move on with life go far! Don't go it alone. Enlist the help of others. Reach out. Have a goal, a plan, and a dream. Dreams do come true!

During your military career, did you ever have another Black woman as a mentor?

Yes. Her name was SFC Goines-Audrey. She was the Non-Commissioned Officer in Charge of one of the clinics in my unit at the Schofield Barracks Health Clinic, Hawaii. She was not in my direct chain of command, but we saw each other probably daily. During that time, I was a Sergeant, so she really didn't have to converse with me, but she always encouraged me to press forward.

What was your experience like (or lack of experience) with a Black woman as a mentor?

SFC Goines-Audrey was a great leader in her own right. She reached out to me when I needed help the most. Although she was not in my direct chain of command, she took the time to help me in my process of applying to the AMEDD Enlisted Commissioning Program (AECP). She had already gone through the process and for whatever reason did not go, but she still reached out on my behalf. For that, I am truly grateful. She could have thrown everything away and been bitter but she helped her fellow Sister-in-Arms along the way. Before she brought the program to my attention, I didn't know it (AECP) existed. Even now when I see that a Soldier is getting out or wants to change his or her career path, I make sure he or she knows about the AECP program and help them in any way I can.

What would you tell other Black women who serve about taking on the role of a mentor to other Black women serving?

I feel it is very important to seek another Black woman currently serving or Veteran Black woman as a mentor, especially if she came through the same career path. The nursing field is much different than say Human Resources; therefore, job related/job specific things will only make sense to someone in that same line of service. I am not saying that if you find a mentor in another line of work that they cannot be helpful. They can, by all means! We should also seek out the opportunity to mentor other Black women serving behind us because they are our future. When we retire or exit the service, who will they have to rely on and be encouraged by?

10

Working with Patience and Perseverance to Achieve Your Goals

KESHIA HUGHSTON

I know how you feel, believe me. I've felt the same way at times. I mean, it's never just one thing; it's never just a single issue or problem or challenge we find ourselves facing. There are moments on this journey when it feels like the hard times continuously mount, but pursuing our path one step at a time is all we're required to do. If we can push past our reliance on self and become open to receive God's promises, He will strengthen our stride and give us what we need each day, each step of the way.

I remember the days back at the barracks during basic training, hanging around with some of my newfound friends and acquaintances. For some reason, Sundays stand out in my mind. Even if I close my eyes right now and think back, I can see us sitting around trying to enjoy the day talking about family and friends back home and sharing some of the hope we thought this place would bring to each of us. I can see the sun is shining bright and I can feel its warmth. There's a sort of haze over those days but not a dimming shadow that takes away from its pleasantness. No, it's more of a sepia tone that seems to color my memory and create a familiar frame somewhat like the significance and fondness relegated to an old family photo and keepsake.

Sundays just seemed calmer and not simply because we weren't running around at the crack of dawn going for a few miles run or wearing our backsides raw on those flimsy Army-green mats alternating push-ups and sit-ups at two minute intervals. Honestly, the training was one of the best parts of the military experience for me. I was challenged physically in a way that I had ever experienced. So, besides the time of day we trained, 4:45 a.m. formation and with less than adequate equipment at times, I really couldn't complain. All the physical training we endured certainly paid off and got me into the best shape of my life. I wasn't a couch potato or anything when I went in. I was pretty lean and accustomed to working out at the gym, but I wasn't a great runner for any speed or distance, and I could barely do a single push-up. So the warm morning air down at Fort Jackson, even in the winter months made running around in t-shirts and shorts in our new outdoor gymnasium more than bearable.

But as I said, Sundays were different. Sure, we did workout sometimes, especially if we weren't doing so well with the run or pushups. I was regularly at the front of the line asking for extra help from some of the other trainees who were much better at one thing or the other. It was so nice to pull together and help each other the way we did. We'd do pushups each night and challenge one another so we could build our strength. Being physically capable was an important aspect and expectation in the role of a Soldier and, I would argue, should be just as important whether in the armed forces or not. Passing the PT test was a requirement if we wanted to graduate basic training, and there was no way I was going to fail. I wasn't going to let myself down and not finish what I started or at least make my very best effort to succeed. That's honestly always been the mindset I've worked hard to maintain about things: to try my very best, to give my very best.

Sundays were different because they moved slower and always presented what seemed a disproportionate amount of undistracted time. There seemed to be too much time to think and replay the scenes of past scenarios and debate the choices and decisions I had made that led me to those days of sitting around in Army fatigues with the rest of my platoon. The day was really my own for the most part and so were the choices that got me there.

I sometimes thought to myself how different the military experience might have been if I had chosen to be more patient in joining the Army and given myself the time to put together my officer candidacy package. However, patience was not something I had mastered in those days and is something I still sometimes struggle today. I just wanted to be gone. I had no time to waste or wait. I needed to get away, and sooner rather than later. I wanted space and time to think about my life and my fragile marriage.

Was I really ready to honor my vows and be the good Christian wife people expected me to become? Was I really ready to settle down and make choices for the rest of my life that included the consideration of someone else? I certainly thought I was when I said *I do*, but the reality was far less acceptable. My future felt so uncertain. I felt like I was walking in the dark most of the time. Sure, there were moments of light, but for the most part, the path forward seemed dim and lonely with little hope. I battled with these feelings since my earliest days in college. Admittedly, back then I didn't know what to call it. I mean I don't ever recall anyone in my family talking about this thing known as depression, even though the symptoms were obviously there for a number of my loved ones.

I did say the challenges kept coming, right? I was not only contending with these internal mental health dilemmas and questions about my marriage and future, but I was also battling the tests that came from my new position in the military. I entered basic training with my bachelors degree from Penn State, so I was immediately given the rank of E4 and the unfamiliar responsibility of serving as the platoon leader. This prompted even more questions. What was I doing there leading and having the responsibility of group exercises and movements for these people? What made me think I had what it took to work closely and one on one with my drill sergeants and other leaders who had been there for so many years? Why should the members of my platoon (some of whom were older, men, and from other races) listen to my orders? "Who does this little Black girl think she is?" I once overheard someone say. "I hate taking orders from niggers," someone else remarked under his breath. I saw the defiance and annoyance in their faces at times; I saw the disapproval in the eyes of some.

And let me not forget to mention the disdain and what I later learned was jealousy I experienced at the hand of one of my female drill sergeants – a Black woman who served many years alongside her husband, who somehow was able to work in the same training group. Most said they were an unlikely couple; she was not as attractive as some thought she should be for a husband as well put together and handsome as he was. It was really not my business until he made it mine by taking every opportunity he could to flirt with me and get me alone in his office with my battle buddy Robin. Sure, Robin tried to tell me that he was interested in me, but we were both married and I was a Soldier in basic training, meaning I was off-limits to my superiors. Not only this, but I had heard of his reputation with the other female Soldiers – a reputation of which his wife was also well aware.

I did a lot a self-talk in those days, probably just as much as I do now. But I think it was one of those Sunday afternoons in basic training that I became acutely aware of the fact that it was happening and, more importantly, what I was actually saying to myself. Why was I repeating the same defeated and negative talk that some of those around me expressed? Why were the questions I asked myself so riddled with doubt and a lack of confidence? This had to stop! I asked myself what choice I had. This was the job, this was the place my choices led me, and this was the challenge set before me. I heard this message one day loud and clear, and I know it was from the Lord. I was new in my Christian faith. I had only come to Jesus about six months before I got married, and here I was not even a year into my marriage and I had run away to this place. I remember feeling alone and isolated at first, feeling like I had made the worst mistake of my life. So, I did what you're supposed to do as a good Christian; I tried to get to know my God. I read my Bible each night and took advantage of the down time on Sundays to attend church service so I could learn. It was not only here in the Good Book and the house of worship that I found words of encouragement and scripture to remind myself in moments of weakness and despair. It was also in the people He placed in my midst. His people. His children.

I never expected to gain so much in those eight weeks, and for a time, I thought I would just be there *marking time* doing nothing but waiting to get to my next duty station. However, I knew enough to know that I needed something greater, something more than *me* and I was grateful that I sought it! I had done an amazing job of proving to myself that I just wasn't strong enough to get through this life on my own. I was exhausted and wanted some of that power and energy my former college guidance counselor and mother away from home Dr.

Kharem talked about. I needed to be able to lean on something more than my own intellect, my own desired path, my own will and strength. I tried to do my part in this new relationship with Jesus and He gave back to me so much more than I could imagine. He opened my eyes to the fact that His plan was to use this place and my choices for my benefit. I'm reminded of scripture where it says, "And we know that in all things God works for the good of those who love him, who are the called according to His purpose" (Romans 8:28). I grew to love God, and He filled me with a hope and confidence unlike I had ever experienced.

As a result, I experienced a shift in paradigm and a change in my worldview. A determination came over me and I resolved that I would approach each new experience and challenge in the same way: small, manageable actions and daily choices that could contribute to success at the end. I was assured that just like the people God placed around me to encourage and strengthen me through the physical and emotional challenges I faced in basic training, I could expect this same care and support from Him each time, giving me the resources and relationships my life required. He wants me to be victorious and strong in the power of His might (Ephesians 6:10). I learned I no longer needed to tire from trying to carry myself or doubt my ability and worth. I sought the help and comfort in the Holy Spirit (John 14:16) and found the strength I needed daily for myself and to share with those around me.

My Sundays, even long after basic training, serve as a day of reflection and replenishment. My military experience is a milestone of transformation in my life and has paved the way for the work I seek to accomplish today. I was there in that place marking time but eventually there was a wait in readiness for something more to occur, for what God had in store for me and my future. This time marked my life for the better and God transformed this place into one in which I found refuge, healing, and clarity of purpose.

During your military career, did you ever have another Black woman as a mentor?

As a Chaplain's Assistant in the U.S. Army, I was fortunate to have another Black female serve as my mentor through the experience. I knew I had a lot more to learn about my new role as part of the Unit Ministry Team (UMT) and much more about the Chaplains and the military installation in which we would serve. I needed to learn to strike a balance in my dual and at times intimidating role of protector to my non-combatant status Chaplain and also managing the various religious support matters for the Soldiers and surrounding community. Yet I learned a valuable lesson throughout basic training that I carried with me to my first official day of duty, and that is that God will give me what I need when I need it.

What was your experience like (or lack of experience) with a Black woman as a mentor?

Angela Grimes, a fellow Chaplains Assistant having already given more than a decade of service by the time we met gladly embraced her newly added God-given role as my mentor, accountability partner, and friend. She was funny, creative, and loyal, and she loved the Lord. Her calm and even-keeled demeanor never gave room for angst or strife in juggling the day-to- day expectations the role demanded. She modeled a leadership and management style that I still carry with me today.

She treated me as a member of the team and never as a subordinate for her to rank over. She was respectful, collaborative, and integral, and she was always one to assume positive intent. She was fearless and smart with a discerning spirit, and she was well connected to other encouraging Black females in the military. I truly felt cared for and surrounded by support throughout my time of service.

What would you tell other Black women who serve about taking on the role of a mentor to other Black women serving?

If you have the opportunity to be a winning example for another female Soldier, or if you're in the place I found myself, I would encourage you to first pray that the Lord send you what you need and then allow yourself to be available to those placed around you. Come equipped with a discerning heart and a willingness to put down the competitive spirit, and embrace the exponential power of partnership and mentoring.

11

Remain True to Yourself

LUVINA SABREE

I spent all four of my high school years in JROTC and I knew that I wanted to join the military. I was supposed to join the Air Force with my friend on the buddy program, but she got cold feet and decided not to join. At the last minute I decided to join the Army instead. At the time I was only 16 and would not reach my 18th birthday for a couple of years. I really wanted to go but was unable to join unless my mother signed the paperwork for me to join. I think that was one of the best and hardest decisions that my mother made for me. It was hard growing up in the inner city and not having any direction, money for college, or a mentor to direct your path. For me, the military was the only way out of the inner city.

I came from the inner city, and I did not get a chance to experience life much outside of it. I remember preparing to leave for basic training, and it did not hit me nor my mother that I was actually leaving and not coming back until the Army Recruiter came and we had to say goodbye! The only thing that kept going through my mind was a song by Luther Vandross and Dionne Warwick, "How Many Times Can We Say Goodbye." I cried and she cried, but I knew that I had to be strong because I wanted better for myself.

Initially when I joined the Army, I wanted to stay in for 20 years. Basic training and Advanced Individual Training (AIT) was not as bad as I thought it would be. I was excited to go overseas to Germany to my first duty station. I met people from all over. I was excited about the Army and about life! One of the challenges that I experienced on an individual level while at my first duty station was to remember that I was on my own and no longer had a curfew although I was only 17. I remember walking home from the club at around 3:00 a.m., and all of a sudden I got nervous because I thought that I was going to get in trouble for coming home late. After catching myself, I remembered that I did not have my mother to go home to and that I was on my own. Another thing that came to mind was that although I did not have my mother putting restrictions on me, I still needed to live by some rules. Here are the rules that I came up with: I will remain a lady at all times. I will not use profanity. I will not smoke cigarettes or drink alcohol. I will not become promiscuous, and I definitely will not mess around with a married man.

The biggest problem I had in the Army was a lack of leadership from both men and women. I remember one incident that occurred after formation. One NCO from my platoon told me to pick up the cigarette butt he had just thrown on the ground, and I told him that I was off. He took it up with my Platoon Sergeant (who had given me the afternoon off), our acting Commander, who was a 1LT, and our First Sergeant. I was put on 14 days extra duty and restricted to the base. When my Commander arrived back at the unit and he had seen me cleaning up after duty hours, he asked why. When I explained to him that I did not pick up cigarette butts after the Sergeant threw one down and told me to pick them up, he immediately called all parties involved into his office and said, "I hope that this Soldier is lying about why she is on extra duty." Once they confirmed that I was on extra duty for not picking up his cigarette butt after I was released from duty, my Commander was hot! I was told in front of them that my extra duty ended now! I was then asked to leave the office.

The next morning in formation, the company was informed that non-smokers no longer had to police call cigarettes and when you are giving Soldiers orders, they had to make sure they were not abusing their authority. When I went to my Platoon Sergeant and told him that the Sergeant had thrown the cigarette butt down in front on me and then told me to police call the area after he had given me time off, he told me that I had disobeyed a lawful order and that was why he didn't support me. I felt so hurt. In my mind, I couldn't get this straight. I asked my Platoon Sergeant, "Any Sergeant can come up to me when I am off duty and give me an order to do something and I am supposed to do it?" and he said "yes." That was one of the turning points in the Army for me. I am glad that I had a Commander that was prior enlisted that saw straight through what that Sergeant had done to me.

I respected him because he stood up for what was right after his subordinates had made a bad decision. The others didn't see that he had tried to belittle me in front of his friends. They didn't see that he was abusing his authority. The only thing they could see was what I did not do. I was never loud or disrespectful to the Sergeant. If I could do this all over again, I would have sought after a Sergeant who was fair and understood the Army better. My advice to anyone who finds herself in a similar situation would be to learn your place as a Soldier and learn the regulations. If you are ever in a situation where you feel you are being mistreated, find a squared-away Sergeant that will guide you in the right direction.

Another challenge I experienced in the military that remains difficult for me to discuss even today is developing relationships with senior/male Soldiers who take advantage of your trust. I will not go into full details because it is still too painful to discuss, but I write this with the hope that it will help someone. It is okay for you to befriend a male Soldier. What's not okay is him taking advantage of that friendship by forcing you to touch him inappropriately. It is not okay for him to make you feel uncomfortable because you do not want to do something. Being afraid and feeling like you are alone if you find yourself in a situation like this is normal – but you are NOT alone. There are others who have been in this situation and survived. The key is to get help. Please seek help. You are never alone when someone violates your trust in this manner.

I never expected to experience this type of challenge before joining the military because I was Christian. I never thought that I would change my religion. In 1990, I started to learn about Islam. I never played with God, so I wanted to learn more about the religion to see if it was something that I really wanted to do. After a year of studying, I decided that this was something that I wanted to do and took my Shahada (declaration of faith). Muslims do not eat pork and there was not adequate non-pork food for me to eat, so I went to the Chaplain to request separate rations. Separate rations is money that you receive from the Army to accommodate a special diet. Upon being approved by the Chaplain for separate rations, I was told by the Chaplain, "I don't want to see you in the mess hall eating ham sandwiches and pork chops." I thought that was one of the most insensitive comments that has ever been made to me as a Muslim. I would expect a comment like that from a fellow Soldier, but from the Chaplain? How rude.

Once many of my comrades learned that I had become Muslim, they pulled away from me and my leadership treated me differently. I felt hurt and alone, but I knew that Islam was the best decision for me. If you are a Muslim or thinking about becoming a Muslim, or if you practice any religion, please remain true to yourself. I am no longer in contact with many of the people I associated with early on in the Army. But I am still a friend to this day with the people who really meant something to me.

I wanted to give you a small glimpse into my life as a Muslim Soldier and a survivor of whatever was thrown my way. I would like to leave you with a few tips that have helped me throughout life. When bad things happen — and they will happen — find out the lesson in the experience. Don't focus on the bad, but instead ask yourself what were you supposed to learn from the experience? Learn from that experience and keep moving forward. Live life to the fullest. Never be one of those people who say that when they get older, they should have done this and I should have done that. Don't think about it, just do it! There is a wealth of information via the Internet. If someone else has done it, it should be easy for you; if no one has done it, find a way to get it done!

During your military career, did you ever have another Black woman as a mentor?

Yes and no. I had a young Sergeant who tried to mentor me but failed miserably due to a lack of experience and prior mentorship.

What was your experience like (or lack of experience) with a Black woman as a mentor?

When I joined the Army at 17, my grandmother was my example of a mentor prior to me joining the military.

She was fun and loving but firm when she needed to be and always gave the best advice. When I joined the Army, I expected someone to take me under her wing and mentor me, but what I received was the opposite.

I distinctly recall two examples where I lost complete respect for two supervisors. The first example occurred when I was stationed overseas. My NCO took credit for work I had completed while staying late after work. She had a chance to tell the truth and give me credit for doing the extra work, but she chose not to. I told her she had forever lost my respect.

The second example occurred with another supervisor while I was stationed stateside. I experienced the most unprofessional counseling session ever by my supervisor, an older Staff Sergeant. The thought of her still makes me feel bad when I think of her and her (non-existing) leadership.

During a counseling session she was slouched in her chair sitting with her arm hanging off the back of the chair and she asked, "Do you think you are pretty?" I was shocked! Was this supposed to be a professional counseling? She complained about how all the Soldiers only asked for me to help them when they came to the supply room. I asked, "Have I done something wrong?" and she stated "No." So I requested to speak to the First Sergeant. I explained the situation and was transferred to a different section in the company.

Both had an opportunity to teach me and help me as a young Soldier but instead chose not to. This experience was so bad that I wanted to get out of the military.

What would you tell other Black women who serve about taking on the role of a mentor to other Black women serving?

I would tell every Black woman that I came in contact with to love herself! Once you learn to love yourself and realize that you are a special, unique and a remarkable individual, it will be easier for you to love other women who look like you! We need to get rid of the negative thoughts when we see another Sister that is beautiful, confident, and smart. We need to stop thinking she is out to get us. This is a preconceived idea that stems from the physiological trauma that we as Blacks have received since slavery. We all need each other in one way or another, and it is important to be our best selves to each other. My final thought would be to do whatever it takes to have your Soldiers remember you and smile, and say that you were really there for them. Don't act so they remember you with unpleasant thoughts.

12

Activating Your Faith
While Under Pressure

KATHY MARIE CARTER

I finally got to live my childhood dream to join the U. S. Air Force! I remember watching Gomer Pyle when I was young. What I loved most about this show was Sergeant Carter. For starters, I like the name Carter because that's my last name. Sergeant Carter also was very bossy. This show appealed to that side of me that was tired of getting bossed around by adults and other kids in school and in my neighborhood. I couldn't wait to grow up and join the military, because I was going to be the boss and no one would boss me around!

On my first day at Basic Training in San Antonio, Texas, I was in my mid 20s and thought basic training would be a breeze. To my dismay, my first day was like a horror story out of a scary movie. A tall, blue-eyed woman yelled at me. She would get in my face, widen her eyes and yell at the top of her lungs! I freaked out and was frozen in time. I was so angry I wanted to run for the nearest gate and get on the next thing smoking to New Orleans. I wasn't about to take that kind of abuse! But I quickly learned it wasn't abuse, but a way to build cohesiveness in a short period of time. After my first week, I became accustomed to the ways of doing business in Basic Training.

I went from Basic Training to Eglin Air Force Base in Florida. The sun was truly shining and I was full of excitement and great joy. I was ready to begin my new career and a journey that would change my life for the better. My experience on active duty was so much fun. I laughed a lot, sung songs, play cards, danced, and went to church with friends. I had an awesome job, where I got to meet people from various countries and cultures. And another thing, I was less than a 4 hour drive to my hometown. Eglin AFB is where I began to develop lifelong friendships.

During my military career, I held three different jobs. I started out as a Service Specialist, then Air Cargo Specialist, and then Information Management Specialist. I was a reservist that went on active duty multiple times. During the September 11 crisis, I was again called to active duty at Wright Patterson AFB in Ohio.

While on active duty, I began to experience wicked headaches. The pain was so severe that all I could do was rub my head and my temples to try and get quick relief. I'm not one to take medication on a regular basis, but I felt the need to take something. My vision started to become skewed. I would be reading and notice that parts of the words would be missing. Now I'm thinking something was wrong with this book. I got my eyes checked and, low and behold, a pituitary tumor was found. I was rushed to the surgeon. "This thing is huge!" he said. I would have to have surgery right away. I was not moved when I was diagnosed because I had this unshakable feeling in my soul and faith that I would overcome this challenge. Family, friends, co-workers and doctors thought I was crazy, because I believed God and what the Holy Spirit was guiding me to do or not do. This challenge was a true testament of my faith and I welcomed the experience.

The ophthalmologist rushed me off to a young surgeon. The surgeon explained that the tumor was very big and must be removed immediately. I told the surgeon I would pray about surgery, and he told me I don't have time to pray about it. He insisted that I could ask 10 people and they would all tell me the same thing, that surgery was my only option. I put my hands on my hips and told him, "I'm not going to ask

10 people, but I'll ask the Most High God and I'll get back with you." He was very upset with me and I was not happy with his treatment towards me.

That Saturday I went to church. There was a play that day about a man that diagnosed with a disease and the doctor told him he had to have surgery. The man said he would have to pray about it, and the doctor told him he could pray, but still needed that surgery. I was blown away! How could this be, a play that depicts my current situation! I knew it was God reassuring me to do His perfect will.

My co-workers, friends, family and other medical staff attempted to pressure me to make a decision they thought was best for me, but I knew not to listen to man when I knew my answers were coming from a Higher Power. As a Black woman in the military, I knew it would be no easy task, yet I was willing to persevere. The doctor called me day and night, day after day, but I did not have a desire to talk with him. I decided to take leave and go to visit my godmother in Michigan. I needed my family more than ever, and my godmother and her children were there for me. They accepted my decision and supported me all the way.

I found an advocate that would speak on my behalf. I explained to her that I opted not to have surgery and would like to just go about my business and do my job. She said she would have a meeting with the necessary people and get back to me after the meeting. Several days later, she called me around noon and told me the meeting was going to take place at 2:00 p.m. She said it would be best that I represent myself in this matter. Now I knew this wasn't right, but I prepared myself for the meeting. I got to the hospital and there were at least 10 officers there and the hospital attorney. At that time, I was an E-6. I had on my nice blue uniform.

As I began to speak, I felt the power of the Holy Spirit, and I knew I was going to express my thoughts in a clear and concise manner. One of the doctors asked me why I decided not to have surgery and I remember saying, "You know how you know something and you just can't shake it off? Well, that's where I am. This decision is not out of fear, but out of love for myself and my longing to be pleasing unto God." They all leaned back in their chairs and had no more to say. I went back to work, as if nothing had happened, because they weren't sure what to do with me.

Things seemed to be going along without any hardship until I received a restriction letter from a major in my office. He collaborated with the surgeon to put me on driving restrictions. I was outraged! How dare he meddle in my medical affairs! I marched to that hospital so fast.

My heart was racing, sweat was pouring from my face and heat was coming from my body. I was ready for battle! I had a heated conversation with the surgeon and reminded him that my medical records are private. Why would he have a conversation with my co-worker? He said that because I had limited vision, I needed to be placed on restrictions. My heart started aching! At that moment my soul felt so empty, I could have just died. Years earlier, I had driven across every major interstate in the United States. It was one of my greatest joys. I was born to move about on this earth, unrestricted. Now I was bound and shackled all because I made a decision that the surgeon and some other folks did not like.

There I was, having to ask people for a ride to and from work, to dining facilities and restaurants, rides to shop and so forth. I was primarily confined to the Air Force base. I felt that these were not the right actions toward me and was determined to find an answer to make things better for myself. I did. I found information pertaining to being restricted to drive a Private Owned Vehicle, and I was entitled to daily taxi service up to a certain amount. I was thrilled! This was the next best thing to driving. Seek and you will find!

144

Riding in a taxi was as close to driving as I would get, and I was fine with it. The sun started shining brighter, the birds sung louder and the wind blew softer. My experience had become better.

Then, I was back in Minot, North Dakota, and back on Reserve status. I decided to accept an active duty position at Minot Air Force Base. Things were going along very well. It was a new career field for me, but I became acclimated quickly. But months later, I got sick. I was with friends and I was eating everything in sight. They asked me why was I eating so much, but I couldn't give them a good answer because I didn't know why I was eating so much. Later that night, I went to sleep only to wake up around 4:00 a.m. with an extremely bad headache. My head hurt so bad that I could hardly see. I called my friends and asked them if they had something for a headache. I got to their house and started throwing up. They ended up taking me to the hospital twice. The first time, I was diagnosed with a headache. The second time I went to the hospital because I had lost my sight.

My military career was in jeopardy. I was not ready to get out, but I knew there was a chance I might have been discharged before I was ready to retire. After going to the Medical Board at Lackland AFB in San Antonio, Texas, the board members thought it best to discharge me with an Honorable Discharge. I was so upset I cried in the courtroom. I cried when I got to my hotel room and all throughout the night. I knew I could do my job, so why would they discharge me? My emotions were all over the place and life seemed so depressing to me. I knew that God had to have something greater in store for me, but I still wanted to continue my career in the military. I started listening to a Celine Dion song called "A New Day Has Come" and a new day it was. I started to give thanks for my military experience and embrace what was happening, because I knew God had other things in store for me.

Now, I am enjoying life as a holistic body worker, speaker, and life coach. I travel often, visiting friends and family, as well as doing speaking engagements. I inspire, encourage and help women to listen to that small quiet voice and help them to take the courageous and loving actions that they believe are best for them. Many will tell you what to do and how to do things, but I encourage you to always pray about everything and let the Holy Spirit be your guide, and remember to not make your decisions out of fear, because fear has torment. Instead, make all your decisions out of love and you will always make good decisions.

This experience was very challenging for me, but I knew that I wasn't alone. I knew that God was with me through it all and He's still with me. This soulful experience is one that I would not change for the world. I learned so much and grew by leaps and bounds. It was truly a test of my faith.

During your military career, did you ever have another Black woman as a mentor?

Yes I had a mentor, but she disappeared after day one. She picked me up at the airport, introduced herself and started schooling me. She told me what I should do and what not to do. In essence, she told me what she thought I needed to know. Yet I was blessed with a great First Sergeant and he was the one that was more like a mentor to me than my one-day mentor. He was a very generous and kind man. He made life easy for me and I greatly appreciated him and still do to this day.

What was your experience like (or lack of experience) with a Black woman as a mentor?

She was a mean-spirited person. I felt like I was a bother to her and she didn't want anything to do with me. When we got to the base, she dropped me off at the lodging facility and took off. I think I saw her a few times after that first day, but that was it when it came to a mentor.

What would you tell other Black women who serve about taking on the role of a mentor to other Black women serving?

I would encourage Black women to be open to a new Sister coming into the military. I would also encourage her to be understanding and supportive, so that this Sister can start her career with ease and on solid ground.

It's like going to school as a kindergartener for the first time and you don't know a soul. You're afraid, you don't know what to expect, and you're the new kid on the block. Having a mentor that is loving, kind, and supportive can make all the difference in the world, especially pertaining to a Sister's military career. Mentoring can create strength and courage to withstand many obstacles that are bound to happen.

Like that kindergartener, those women will look back on their entrance into the military with great memories and appreciation for having a mentor and the positive difference it made in their lives. As Black women, we need each other, especially those who are in the military.

MENTORSHIP

"I've learned that people will forget what you said, people will forget what you did, but people will never forget how you made them feel."

- Dr. Maya Angelou

13

Believe In Yourself
When All Others Fail You

TAMARA THOMAS-SANFORD

My military experience started in 1997, when I was assigned to Fort Jackson, South Carolina for basic training, then, later, to Fort Lee, Virginia for advance initial training (AIT). I enlisted at the age of 17 and received my first permanent duty assignment to Wurzburg, Germany (67th Combat Support Hospital), shortly after turning 18. My first assignment began my journey of the many ups and downs that I would face during my military career. Reality then hit me: not only did I feel alone, but physically, as a Black woman, I was actually alone, in a foreign country, property of the United States Army.

When I arrived in Frankfurt, Germany (early 1998), my supposed "mentor" met me at the airport. Let the journey begin! I was thankful to have traveled overseas with a battle buddy that was also assigned with me in

AIT. He had experienced life at a much greater capacity than me, and was fearless. We became really good friends, and he helped me push through some of my very difficult spurts in the beginning half of my tour in Germany. Living in a foreign country, I often felt alone, lost, and fearful of the unknown. During this time, there were some highs, but far too many lows, and having a battle buddy was key.

As a young Soldier, I thought I would receive guidance and direction from those assigned to lead me. Instead, my NCO "mentor" felt as if she had mind control over me, and could make or break my career. One minute she would make it appear as if she cared and wanted me to succeed; the next minute, she would leave me hanging to fend for myself. I was a young soldier, and, at the time, I was very easily upset. My NCOs knew how to push all the right buttons to get a negative reaction out of me, which led to various forms of reprimands. As a defense, I began to build walls and became withdrawn towards my senior female leaders. However, I knew I had to learn how to practice self-control in an effort to maintain my military bearing, despite how I may have felt on the inside.

With all of the negative barriers this early in my career, I had no clue about what to expect from the military, or what the military was supposed to expect from me. I was confused about my identity – who I was as a person, a Soldier, and, most importantly, a Black woman. I wasn't sure where I fit in with my new world or how to overcome my doubts and fears. I wasn't sure if I even had a voice, and, if I did, how I could stay true to Tamara even in the midst of all the change that was taking place in my life. I was completely lost for months; I was lost in my identity, lost in my abilities to be a great Soldier, and lost in my faith (which didn't become strong until much later in life). All I knew was that I wanted more than what was being offered; I felt that life could be better than what I was projecting. At this time, I knew I would have to plow my way through self-doubt, climb the hill of lack of confidence, push through my thoughts of not being successful, and overcome my fears to one day be a leader in the U.S. Army. I also knew that overcoming these things wouldn't be easy. After all, I had no one willing to take me under her wing and step up to the plate of mentorship.

Here I am, an 18-year-old Black woman in Europe with the desire to do my best, be better than my worst and move forward in a positive light. So, where did I go from there? To whom should I turn, and in which direction should I go? When I have that lack of confidence, to whom should I talk about my intimate fears and concerns, and from where do I seek the answers when I'm lost or unsure? I was thousands of miles away from family (with only one familiar face from the United States), and surrounded by a different culture with only a few people and Soldiers that resembled me. I was so confused with trying to figure out who was truly leading and who should I follow. As much as I wanted to fight the feeling, once again, I was completely lost in myself and in my ability to be a successful Soldier, now leader. Surrounded by predominately male Soldiers and leaders with a Caucasian female "mentor," I had to figure out my next move, and I had to figure it out quickly.

Time passed, I continued to learn and adjust to life in the military, and, before long, I was moving up the ranks into leadership positions. As I embarked in the world of leadership, I had to figure out how to lead versus how to follow. I had to figure out what made an exceptional leader and how to develop what leadership style worked best for me. I believe that when God created me, He created me to be a leader! After all, I was my mom's oldest child, and when the time came to step up with my brothers and sister, I did it with full force. Through all of my fears, self-doubt, and indifference, the desire to lead and take charge was still very prevalent, and I knew I had to take the necessary steps on my own to be successful. This journey came with a whole different set of trials and I would have to, once again, walk through the valleys, plow through the hills, climb the mountain tops and fight various battles with my two-man Army (me and the Good Lord). I pulled myself up by my bootstraps, regained focus, and realized that the reason I entered into the military was far more important than the negative energy clogging the air around me.

Later on that year, I became very close with another battle buddy, who is still my very good friend today. I know God placed her in position for us to be there for each other and to help one another through some of the not-so-pleasant times. I was so relieved that I finally had someone (a peer) that I could identify with physically: a female Soldier that actually wanted more and who cared. I was grateful that she understood me, and that I had someone with whom I could share my struggles, fears, doubts and my desire to want to move forward in my career. She was on fire from the time she stepped foot on ground and was always determined to be her best, and accomplish every single task given to her. We traveled the rest of my tour in Germany together and, within two and a half years, I was promoted to Sergeant. She, too, became very successful in her military career. As I began to mature, I realized that in life, it was imperative that I surround myself with individuals that were positive. It was important that my peers be Soldiers who were also striving to succeed and be leaders!

My promotion, however, didn't come with an easy road like I thought it would. I was the same rank as my prior NCOs, which caused all sorts of confusion within the section. But because of their time in grade and service, they outranked me, and my female NCO would make sure that she let it be known. In an effort to ease the tension, I was later moved to another job within the same unit. I still didn't have a proper perspective on what a great mentor was, or how a great leader leads, due to my lack of mentorship and examples of leadership during this point in my career. I just hoped that my future experiences would be totally different and more guiding. I thought that I would become closer with my current supervisors, who resembled me as a Black female Soldier. I patiently waited for that day when one of them would call me into their office and care enough to guide me in the right direction. This day eventually came, but the guidance did not come from any of the Black female NCOs that supervised me at the time. By the time I finally received "mentorship," I was very angry and bitter and needed a serious reality check.

It was so difficult for me to balance my leadership responsibilities with the raging emotions I was feeling on the inside for which I had no outlet. However, just when I needed her most, the good Lord finally blessed me with a leader who physically "looked" like me and genuinely cared about me. She knew that I had become bitter, angry, tired, and ready to give up. But, once again, she reminded me that God built me to be a great leader, even before the military, and that I had a greater purpose to fulfill. She reminded me of how far I had come and how much further I still had to go, and that this wasn't the time to throw in the towel or build even higher walls.

I could tell that she saw something greater in me than I could see in myself. But she was a commissioned officer, and did the best she could when she had the time to check on me and speak words of wisdom to me. She expressed how powerful knowledge was and how important it was for me to know the rules and regulations that governed the Army. She encouraged me to read the technical manuals (TMs) and field manuals (FMs) that covered the many job titles that I would fulfill during my career and how important it was to be a master in each of these fields.

One of the most important pieces of advice that she gave me was to always remember my reason for coming into the military in the first place. This advice was so important because my reason for joining, my "why," was so strong and dear to my heart that it would carry me far. When I felt like giving up, when I didn't think it was worth it anymore to move forward, I would just began to focus on my "why" and my overall purpose for joining the Army, and I used those thoughts to help me push through. This concept was very important for me to understand in life in general; it's always important for me to know the reason why I do the things that I choose to do. Once this became prevalent to me, it gave me the willpower to keep marching on, leaving the mess behind, clearing up what was in front of me, and trucking my way toward my destiny!

So, how did I conquer the beginning stages of my military career and move forward toward my destiny? Ultimately, my focus was on doing my best with the little military life experience and maturity that I had, so as to not disappoint my brothers, sister, and my grandparents (especially since I had lost my grandmother early in my career). I now knew and became bold in my "WHY" and wanted to begin to run with it, versus focusing on all the negativity around me. After receiving my promotions, losing my grandma, and being treated so horribly, the loneliness became too real and the depression settled in deeper. I remember experiencing my first real mental breakdown as a Soldier. This was not the end result I wanted. I remember being emotionally unstable many times, but physically I kept on pushing. I knew greater would eventually come and I couldn't give up or give into my fears. This was important because I had my brothers and sister whom I wanted to offer the world to, parents that I wanted to impress, and my guardian angel looking down on me. I wasn't afraid to admit that I needed help, and I sought after different avenues to receive it, outside of my chain of command.

I sought professional counseling in order to stabilize all of my emotions, regain my confidence, and have the willpower to continue to move forward and overcome my inner fears. Counseling was very beneficial for me. It gave me insight and allowed me to sort through the millions of thoughts circulating in my restless mind. However, I knew that there was something deeper inside of me that needed to be fulfilled as well. I began to crave this something deeper and looked to religion and spirituality as a way to fill the void I was feeling. Thus, I had my first "adult" experience with church and spiritual counseling, and this is where I found that inner peace in the Temple of God.

This was the sort of peace that surpassed all of my understanding. The Temple is where I found rest, my joy, and, most of all, I found the will to move on. The Temple is where I learned about God, a higher power and being, and knew that I wasn't walking on this Earth alone. I was thankful for a place to worship, let go and move forward in my life; this new finding began a new journey in my life and opened up many more chapters.

During your military career, did you ever have another Black woman as a mentor?

During the early part of my military career, I didn't have many Black women leaders in my life and the few that I had didn't seem interested in making sure I was "squared away" or on track with my career. Having a positive battle buddy, another individual who wanted to succeed, was my key to success!

What was your experience like (or lack of experience) with a Black woman as a mentor?

After about two and a half years in service I had one Black female Major who could see I was headed down the wrong path. She saw my built-up frustration with the senior Black women in our section. This Major was one of the few who cared enough to pull me into her office, feed me wisdom, and give me knowledge. This helped to tame my firecracker ways, because at this point I was very bitter and closed in, and was too afraid to trust women in general.

What would you tell other Black women who serve about taking on the role of a mentor to other Black women serving?

I believe reaching out to all female Soldiers is very important, because as women we go through so much in life. It's so easy to lose focus and walk in the wrong direction, so guidance is a must. Even deeper, as Black women, not only does it seem as if we are always having to prove ourselves to the world, but it often seems that we are in a battle of proving ourselves to each other. The competiveness is so deep and real, but the desire to want to help each other is so weak. It seems that we are always afraid of the next person doing more and being better, so we compete with each other instead of joining forces to conquer the many trials and tribulations that we face before us. In closing, what's for you will be for you, and what's for someone else will be for that person. Never be afraid to reach out to the youth, pull them up by their bootstraps and help guide them down a positive, healthy path.

14

Breaking Barriers, Pushing Forward and Leaving a Legacy

LENITA CORNETT

A s a young Black girl growing up, I didn't imagine that I would be enlisted in the military successfully serving for over 19 years. I watched my father go to work in his fatigues early in the morning and come home almost when it was time for my family to go to bed. I have a large family consisting of my mother, Betty S. Jenkins, father, Eddie L. Jenkins, Sr. and my five siblings Eddie, Sherman, Lequita (my twin sister), Tamecia and Latoya. I admired my father's military career, especially when I saw him walk with confidence in his uniform. At age 17, on August 30, 1995, I was headed to Basic Training at Fort Jackson, South Carolina. After I completed my Advance Individual Training in Fort Lee, Virginia, I was assigned to 204th Forward Support Battalion (FSB), Fort Hood, Texas. This was my first time being on my own and surrounded by people that I would later have to count on as my military family.

My first duty assignment was a learning experience that made me stronger for my next assignments. My unit was predominantly Black with an equal amount of female and male junior Soldiers. The disparity in the ratio of minority female and male junior and senior leaders was not as evident in my organization. The first year, I was extremely timid, self-conscious, and homesick. I didn't have many friends in my circle. The majority of my Squad Leaders were male and didn't know how to relate to me or encourage me to learn more about personal and professional growth in the military. As a young Black junior Soldier growing up in the military, my perception was that you had to be tough and outspoken or you wouldn't be heard. If you were soft spoken you were considered weak and Soldiers would take advantage of you. So I later developed an attitude to protect myself from people perceiving me as weak. As I continued to mature and feel comfortable in my surroundings, I was then able to see things more clearly; I attended the promotion board for the rank of Sergeant and earned my promotable status. It was later time for me to venture off to my new duty assignment to 4th Squadron, 3rd Armored Cavalry

Regiment, Fort Carson, Colorado. I was a Specialist promotable, ready to take on a leadership role.

Being assigned at Fort Carson was a different experience from Fort Hood. I was in a predominately White organization with a disparity in ratio of female and male Soldiers and Leaders. My supervisor, who was a White female senior Sergeant in rank with over 14 years of service, was biased towards me as soon as I arrived to the unit. I had no sense of direction or guidance when it came to my position or career progression. I had to learn the new culture of being in an aviation unit that no one seemed to care to teach. My promotion to Sergeant was a disaster; neither my supervisor nor my first sergeant or my commander promoted me. I had a fellow Soldier in the rank of Private First Class promote me to Sergeant. This was an ultimate embarrassment to the unit and the Non-Commissioned Officer Corps. Regardless of my circumstance, I continued to focus on the tasks at hand and later reenlisted to be assigned to 203rd FSB, Fort Benning, Georgia.

203rd FSB was a challenge and a great experience for me as a Leader. I learned from the best, both military and civilian logisticians. On Kelly Hill, we worked hard, but we always carried a sense of pride and confidence in authority. I was anxious, but comfortable in my skin. I developed strong working relationships with my peers, seniors and subordinates. I was still eager to learn and grow in my career field. I was impressed with the ratio of Black female leaders that my unit possessed. These leaders were outspoken, aggressive, tough, and proficient in their fields.

As I continued to mature in the military, I was never assigned a mentor to assist me along the way in my journey. I would take the positive things from each leader and place them in my "tool kit" to use when needed. As a Squad Leader and Section Sergeant, many of the challenges I faced were not with my male Soldiers; they were with my female Soldiers. My female Soldiers' response to my orders was disrespectful and, in return, I would counsel them and provide corrective training. I continued to observe their behavior when male leaders would direct them to complete a task. Their response was, at times, noticeably different from how they behaved with me. Now, I was in defense mode and angry. My leadership style was direct and sometimes harsh. I lost my "sensitive side," due to dealing with the culture of the organization and the fast pace of our military operation tempo.

In 2004, it was time once again time for me to move and anticipate a more challenging assignment as Platoon Sergeant with 147th Maintenance Company in

Kitzingen, Germany. When I arrived to my new unit, my First Sergeant welcomed me into my new position as Platoon Sergeant. I was assigned a Platoon of 30 Soldiers with four Squad Leaders (one female). The organization was more of a diverse organization with a mixture in demographics. The learning curve that I had to face was performing two levels up as Platoon Sergeant when I was a Sergeant promotable. The closest to mentorship that I received was my Battalion Command Sergeant Major.

There was a disparity in the ratio of female and male leaders within the company. My fellow Platoon Sergeants were my peers by virtue of my position, but senior in rank. I received their respect and their support in my efforts in the daily operations of our company. As I progressed in my career, I continued to carry on an aggressive behavior that some might have perceived as the "angry Black woman syndrome." I wasn't angry, but for me, that was how I could survive and push forward as I continued to successfully progress in my career. Self-development in civilian and military education was a must, not an option.

In 2006, 147th Maintenance Company was deactivating and it was again time for me to be reassigned to do great things for the U.S. Army. I was then reassigned to Army Sustainment Command, Rock Island Arsenal, Illinois. The majority of the workforce there was composed of senior ranking officers, noncommissioned officers, general schedule (GS) civilians and contractors. My perspective of the military changed as I gained experience working at a strategic level. In my first two years at Rock Island Arsenal, I was assigned as a Material Manager and, later, was locally nominated and selected as an Assistant Inspector General.

In 2011, moving full circle, I was reassigned back to Fort Hood to serve at Headquarters and Headquarters, 13th Sustainment Command (Expeditionary) and Alpha Company, 15th Brigade Support Battalion. In 2013, I began to make my longing for acquiring mentorship a reality. I joined forces and participated with other senior noncommissioned officers on social media to establish an interactive forum that supports women's mentorship for sharing experiences and educating female Soldiers on personal and professional growth. When I pass the torch on to our Army's future leaders, I want to leave a positive impact and inspire Black women who want to serve to know that regardless of their background, education, gender, or race, they will continue to overcome and break barriers and open pathways for female service members to sit along beside their male counterparts as a True Team Member.

LENITA CORNETT

During your military career, did you ever have another Black woman as a mentor?

I had a few African American women as mentors during my military career, but I would say they were not what you would call the traditional mentor. Some were already assigned as my Squad Leader or Supervisor, so it wasn't as if I sought advice from the person of my choice. I would pull something from each of them that made me the leader that I am today. At Fort Hood, Texas, my first duty assignment at 204th FSB (1997-1998), Toni Marsh was one of my Squad Leaders and Section Sergeants when I was in the rank of Private First Class and Specialist. She was tough and candid when she spoke her mind to anyone that came her way. I admired the fact that she took the time to give her experience and opinion in some of my personal affairs that affected me at work. She cared for me and wanted me to be successful in the military as a Soldier, but also a woman.

As I later progressed in the rank of Sergeant (2002-2004), I was introduced to two other African American women that I had the privilege to work with and for: Sharon Gilmore and Valerie Wright. During this time, I was assigned to 203th FSB, Fort Benning, Georgia on

Kelly Hill. Both women were goal setters who accomplished anything they put their minds to do. Through the good and the bad, they both taught me the spirit of resiliency and commitment. Both were great role models when it came to work ethics, higher learning and career progression.

What was your experience like (or lack of experience) with a Black woman as a mentor?

My past experience with Black women as my mentor was not always good, because it wasn't a volunteer basis early in my military career. Early in my career, I didn't understand or have the knowledge of a mentor. If someone would have introduced me to a mentor about fifteen years ago, I think I would have been very intimidated of the thought. Too many times in my career as a young leader and Soldier, it was a struggle to speak or talk to Black women who were senior or equivalent in rank with me. Between the years of 1996-2006, within my assigned organizations, I never saw a group of Black women get along with each other in a personal or professional setting. I don't know if it was because of the intimidation of the rank, position or fear of competition.

LENITA CORNETT

What would you tell other Black women who serve about taking on the role of a mentor to other Black women serving?

I would highly encourage any young woman serving to take on the role of being a mentor to any woman serving. It is important to show a female who is serving the struggles and accomplishments that you have been through so that they have confidence to achieve their goals and continue to break down barriers for our future leaders of tomorrow.

ABOUT THE AUTHORS

LIILA HOLLEY has a heart to help her fellow Veterans. When Lila transitioned from the US Army after 22 years of service, she maneuvered through a battlefield of strong emotions that stalled her progress in the transition process. Lila wondered, *If this was the norm among Veterans, why, then, is no one talking about it?* She took it upon herself to start the conversation about the emotional transition Service Members encounter upon leaving the military.

Lila shares her story of struggle and triumph in her book, *Battle Buddy: Maneuvering the Battlefield of Transitioning from the Military*. Lila offers a first-hand experience of the emotional transition Service Members can expect to encounter when they separate from the military. As the wife of a fellow disabled combat Veteran, and after raising two children in the military, Lila serves as a great resource for military spouses as well.

Lila now enjoys "retired" life in Texas where she resides with her husband and daughter. She continues to serve her community by volunteering in a number of Veteran organizations and as the President of the Killeen Wealthy Sisters Network, a very active women's networking group.

Learn more about Lila at:

www.LilaHolley.com

www.BecomeABattleBuddy.online

ABOUT THE AUTHORS

VERNESSA BLACKWELL, a Veteran's Transition Coach, is a veteran, author and speaker. She believes that you should not wait for a life-shattering moment to propel you into your purpose. Instead, you should be mindful of your future and plan accordingly.

It was during her military career when she learned about the challenges veterans encountered during transition. They often faced feelings of confusion, were unclear about their future, and were unsure of their next steps.

Vernessa's time in this position and her chance encounter with a cancer survivor sparked her purposeful journey into coaching. Although she already had an MBA, several certifications, and experience in the military world, she also became certified as a Transition Joy and Grief Coach.

Vernessa knows that military members battle great trepidation when thinking about their transition. Through her coaching practice, Women Veteran Empowerment, Vernessa instills in her clients the idea that there is more to life than falling effortlessly into a comfortable routine. She imparts upon her clients the importance of making each day meaningful and encourages them to take every available action, so they can live the lives that they have always dreamed of.

To learn more visit:
www.womenveteranempowerment.com

ABOUT THE AUTHORS

★ ★ ★

AMANDA RANDOLPH is a retired Chief Warrant Officer Four Army Veteran of 26 years. Amanda entered the Army as an Intelligence Specialist and progressed through the ranks to Staff Sergeant before transitioning to the Warrant Officer Corps. While on active duty, Amanda was deployed twice to Bosnia Herzegovina in support of Operation Joint Forge and twice to the Middle East in support of Operation Iraqi Freedom.

Amanda is a recipient of the Military Intelligence Corps Knowlton Award for outstanding contributions to Army Military Intelligence. Amanda has a Bachelors of Arts Degree in Intelligence Studies from American Military University and a Masters of Arts in Human

Services Counseling – Marriage and Family from Liberty University.

Amanda currently works as the Family Life Executive Assistant at Strong Tower in Fredericksburg, Virginia. She and her husband, Retired Sergeant First Class Thaddeus Randolph, reside in Fredericksburg with their two sons, Sam, 21, a senior at Virginia State University, and Xavier, 6, a very proud first grader. In her free time, Amanda loves reading, fishing, walking. and spending time with her family.

ABOUT THE AUTHORS

★ ★ ★

PATRICIA WATTS served proudly and honorably for 22 years in the U.S. Army but decided to put her combat boots in the closet and take out her stilettos!

Currently, Patricia serves as the Publisher for HERLIFE DC Metro Magazine. HERLIFE is a national brand magazine published in 8 metropolitan cities. The magazine highlights "Women of Excellence" within the DC Metropolitan community.

Patricia is also the Executive Vice President and Marketing Director for Pacific Culture International (PCI), a pageantry company that hosts one of the largest and fairest pageants on the East Coast. Patricia was bought in to help integrate the Asian American culture into mainstream American.

Patricia has been in the financial industry for 4 years. As a Senior Marketing Director for First Financial Security, Inc (FFS), she believes that if financial literacy is taught while you're young, then financial stability will be part of your livelihood.

Patricia is an active member and former board member of Women Veterans Interactive (WVI), an organization that serves women Veterans at their specific point of need.

Patricia hopes to create an outlet in the DC area for women of all backgrounds to connect and give back to their communities.

ABOUT THE AUTHORS

★ ★ ★

Since 1999 **CATRENA D. FINDLEY** has been on a journey in her military career. Making the decision to join the Army was the toughest and best decisions of her life. She joined the military as a medical specialist and later pursued her dream of becoming a registered nurse.

Catrena is the daughter of Mr. J.B. Lindsey Senior and the late Mrs. Christine Lindsey. She hails from Jackson, Mississippi, where she graduated from William B. Murrah High School. Catrena comes from a large family with two older brothers and two younger half-sisters. Though she was the middle child she always considered herself the matriarch of her siblings because she had lost her mother at the fragile age of nine. This tragedy would later shape the person she is today.

CAMOUFLAGED SISTERS

Catrena is the proud mother and wife to CW4 Eddie L. Findley. Together they are the very proud parents of a blended family that includes nine children.

ABOUT THE AUTHORS

SYLVIA L. McCREA is a retired Chief Warrant Officer Three with twenty-four years of service in the U.S. Army. During her career she served with 3rd Infantry Division (ID), the 101st Airborne Division, the Joint Intelligence Center Pacific in Pearl Harbor, Hawaii, 18th Airborne Corps, 4th Infantry Division, and the Special Operations Command. Sylvia held several leadership positions during her military career, including the Senior Intelligence Analyst in support of OPERATION IRAQI FREEDOM.

Her awards include the Bronze Star, the Defense Meritorious Service Medal, among others. Sylvia has a Bachelors of Arts degree in Psychology from Chaminade University and a Master's of Education in Early Childhood Education from the University of South Florida. She currently works as a government contractor and is the founder and President of ILOW, a disabled-veteran, minority, and women-owned government contracting company based in Tampa, Flordia. Sylvia and her husband, Terry, have one daughter and three sons.

ABOUT THE AUTHORS

SINCERIA ALLEN is a successful real estate broker in Central Texas for over thirteen years in the Bell and Coryell county area. Sinceria is the owner of Triumph Realty Central Texas in the city of Harker Heights Texas for over eight years. It has always been a pleasure to help assist people in purchasing real estate properties. I continue to strive at looking for new approaches to educating people in the community on how to invest in real estate as homeowners or investors.

CAMOUFLAGED SISTERS

KEISHA MOULTON, made the move to Temple, Texas, in 1984 along with her mother and brother. Her mother's short-lived marriage to an Active Duty Army Soldier resulted in her family relocating to the Killeen-Fort Hood area where she resides today.

After graduating from C.E. Ellison High School, in May 1998, Keisha enlisted in the U.S. Air Force at the age of 17. She completed her Basic Military Training at Lackland Air Force Base, San Antonio, Texas, and went on to Technical School Training in Sheppard Air Force Base, Wichita Falls, Texas. She also served as a Health Services Management Journeyman. Keisha is the proud mother of two daughters, Michelle and Vivien. She holds an Associates of Arts in Business Administration, and recently earned a Bachelors of Arts in Marketing.

★ ★ ★

SHIRLEY LaTOUR is a native of Ft Wayne, Indiana and lives here in Killeen, Texas by way of military. She is married and has two children who are 16 and 10. Years old. She graduated from the University of Mary Hardin-Baylor with her Bachelors of Science in Nursing and is licensed and board certified as a Medical-Surgical Registered Nurse. She has been in the healthcare field for over 17 years providing quality care to Soldiers, their dependents, retirees, and civilians. She is also a Certified Health Coach.

Her passion is helping others realize their dream of good health inside and out without conventional medicine. She believes that God placed everything we need for good health here on earth and uses natural supplements to help bring the body back to optimum health. She does assessments, prepares meal plans, provides health coaching, and offers natural supplements in order to get you on your way back to health! Weight management programs are also available. She is always willing to reach out to others in need of physical, spiritual, or financial health. She is an avid volunteer in the Killeen, Belton, and Temple areas and wants to expand her reach around the world!

To learn more visit www.shirleylatour.com

ABOUT THE AUTHORS

KESHIA HUGHSTON is a senior executive human resources professional with nearly 20 years of experience in matters affecting human relations in business and organizations. She has successfully established partnerships and mutually beneficial collaborations and connections in professional and personal relationship settings.

Keshia continues to exhibit her passion for people and relationships as the founder and lead partner of her newly formed organization, Naked Truth Living, LLC, which is a company with aspirations of helping people take an honest and revealing look at themselves and their relationships both personally and professionally. The organization stands on the premise that an enriched and fulfilling existence can be a reality; that abundant living can become a standard for daily living; and that *revealing, healing & inspiring* the truth about of our experiences comprise the foundation necessary to equip and empower people for personal and professional growth in the present and future. The company will serve as a resource to assist its clients in actualizing meaningful change and growth in their relationships and life.

Keshia served as a Chaplain's Assistant in the US Army. She also holds a Bachelors of Arts in English from Pennsylvania State University and an MBA from Eastern University in St. David, Pennsylvania.

For more information visit nakedtruthliving.com

ABOUT THE AUTHORS

★ ★ ★

Described by friends as the only Queen Worker Bee that they know, **LUVINA SABREE** is living her life to the fullest! Luvina is the wife to a retired Army Veteran and a mother of six. She is also an Army Veteran, Registered Nurse, former wholesale car dealer, and an avid maker of soap, bath, body, and hair products.

Luvina is also the organizer of the Killeen's Happy 2 B Nappy (H2BN) Hair Group. H2BN started in November 2005 and has been holding Natural Hair Day (NHD) monthly meetings for 10 years. At each meeting, Luvina teaches the members how to properly maintain their natural hair, how to make natural products, and the importance of eating organically. In 2011, Luvina expanded the meetings by creating the Armed Forces

Natural Hair & Health Expo, which celebrates NHD on a larger scale. www.afnhhe.com

Luvina and her family are also the proud owners of the first full-service organic restaurant in the Killeen area called So Natural Organic Restaurant & Market. At So Natural we cater to the paleo, gluten free, vegan and vegetarian diets and offer healthy, prepackaged meals on the go.

Learn more at www.sonaturalmarket.com

ABOUT THE AUTHORS

KATHY MARIE CARTER is an expert in inspiring and helping women to heal and transform from the inside out. She works with women pertaining to matters of the heart, helping them go from a wounded heart to one that is happy and joyful heart. She helps women to get in touch with their spirits, their souls and bodies, and to release old patterns, habits and thoughts that do not serve them.

Kathy travels all over the country supporting, inspiriting, teachings and coaching women. She works with women one-on-one and in group settings. She also speaks on multiple platforms online and offline, inspiring women to action.

Since Kathy retired from the U.S. Air Force in 2004 as a Master Sergeant, she has been free to build another career as an inspirational speaker, teacher, and life coach. Kathy has her Bachelors of Arts in General Studies, from Minot State University, Minot and is currently living in Houston, Texas.

ABOUT THE AUTHORS

TAMARA THOMAS-SANFORD is a Retired Iraqi War Veteran whom served in the U.S. Army for approximately 10 years. Now a dedicated mother of three and a wife, she overcame major a crossroads in life after being medically released from Active Duty. After struggling with identity, motherhood, becoming a wife, and no longer being a Soldier, she found her passion. Now the owner of a party and event planning business named Believe (Lifestyle Party & Events), her mission is to enjoy life. She continues to adjust as she transitions from Soldier to "Civilian" to Business Owner.

Tamara's passion is helping others to value and enjoy life's most precious moments, by living in the moment. She enjoys hosting themed events throughout the year for the local community that feature local artist and musicians. These themed events give the community a common place to come and enjoy life, build new friendships and business associations, and make lasting memories. Tamara also gives back to various local organizations throughout the year, by sponsoring elementary school children during Christmas, throwing high school graduation parties, and providing meals for families during the Holidays, including the local Veterans of Foreign Wars (VFW).

ABOUT THE AUTHORS

In May 1995, **LENITA F. CORNETT, B.S., DSL, LSSBB(C)** graduated from Rayville High School, Louisiana, and followed in her father's footsteps when she enlisted into the U.S. Army, where she served as an Automated Logistical Specialist. As a "military brat" growing up, diversity, education, and self-development were always her passions. Her hobbies include singing, dancing, listening to music, networking, and building relationships with men and women in diverse areas of business.

To feed her long desire for mentorship, in 2013, Lenita joined forces with a group of active duty female Senior Noncommissioned Officers to provide mentorship forums to junior Soldiers and Leaders through social media.

In 2014, Lenita collaborated with the Women's Mentorship Network providing over 18 years of her experience to active duty females enlisted, officers, and civilians.

In July 2014, Lenita was selected to serve as the Company First Sergeant for Alpha Company, 15th Brigade Support Battalion, 2nd Armored Brigade Combat Team, in Fort Hood, Texas. Lenita is truly a role model; in 2014-2015 she was recognized and inducted by the National Association of Professional Women as its VIP Woman of the Year Circle.

REFERENCES

1. http://usatoday30.usatoday.com/money/econ omy/2011-02-17-womenvets17_ST_N.htm

2. https://en.wikipedia.org/wiki/Crab_mentality

3. http://www.forbes.com/sites/lisaquast/2011/0 4/11/the-struggle-for-female-veterans-to-transition-into-civilian-jobs/2/

WE WANT TO HEAR FROM YOU!!!

If this book has made a difference in your life
Lila would be delighted to hear about it.
Leave a review on Amazon.com!

BOOK LILA TO SPEAK AT YOUR NEXT EVENT!

Send an email to: booking@publishyourgift.com

Learn more about Lila at:
www.LilaHolley.com
www.BecomeABattleBuddy.online

FOLLOW LILA ON SOCIAL MEDIA

 Lila.Holley   CoachLilaHolley

"EMPOWERING YOU TO IMPACT GENERATIONS"
WWW.PUBLISHYOURGIFT.COM

CPSIA information can be obtained
at www.ICGtesting.com
Printed in the USA
BVOW03s2338251116
468713BV00008B/84/P